The European Monetary System: Recent Developments

By Horst Ungerer, Owen Evans, Thomas Mayer
and Philip Young

International Monetary Fund
Washington, D.C.
December 1986

Library of Congress Cataloging-in-Publication Data

The European monetary system.

  (Occasional paper, ISSN 0251-6365 ; no. 48)
  Prepared by H. Ungerer and others, of the European
Department.
  Bibliography: p.
  1. Money—European Economic Community Countries.
I. Ungerer, Horst.   II. International Monetary Fund.
European Department.   III. Series: Occasional Paper
(International Monetary Fund); no. 48.
  HG930.5.E86863 1986   332.4'5'094   86-21432
  ISBN 0-939934-79-5

Price: US$7.50
(US$4.50 university libraries, faculty members, and students)

Address orders to:
External Relations Department, Publications Unit
International Monetary Fund, Washington, D.C. 20431

Contents

The following symbols have been used throughout this paper:

. . . to indicate that data are not available;

— to indicate that the figure is zero or less than half the final digit shown, or that the item does not exist;

– between years or months (e.g., 1984–85 or January–June) to indicate the years or months covered, including the beginning and ending years or months;

/ between years (e.g., 1985/86) to indicate a crop or fiscal (financial) year.

''Billion'' means a thousand million.

Minor discrepancies between constituent figures and totals are due to rounding.

Prefatory Note

This study reviews developments in the European Monetary System from the beginning of 1983 to August 1986; it updates and complements an earlier study prepared by staff members of the International Monetary Fund and published as Occasional Paper No. 19, which covered the time period from the inception of the European Monetary System to the end of 1982.

Like the earlier study, the present study limits itself to a discussion of the evolution of the system and of exchange rate developments and to an analysis of exchange rate variability and economic convergence. The authors are aware that there are other important issues that remain for future work. These include the role of exchange rate policy in fostering domestic economic adjustment, a more detailed analysis of the international competitiveness of EMS countries, and the evolution of the private ECU and its implications for the functioning and further development of the EMS.

Like Occasional Paper No. 19, this paper was prepared in the European Department. The authors benefited from a great number of helpful comments and suggestions made by colleagues in their own and other departments of the International Monetary Fund. Research assistance by Behrouz Guerami of the European Department and editorial help by David Driscoll of the External Relations Department are gratefully acknowledged. The views expressed in this paper represent those of the authors and not necessarily those of the Fund.

I Introduction

The European Monetary System (EMS) came into operation in March 1979, in accordance with the Resolution of December 5, 1978 of the European Council, composed of the Heads of State and Government of the then nine member countries of the European Communities (EC).[1] The objective was to create "a zone of monetary stability in Europe," comprising "greater stability at home and abroad." The founding fathers of the EMS intended that after two years the system should proceed to a second, final phase in which it would be given a more definite institutional framework, in particular through the creation of a European Monetary Fund. This timetable proved unachievable for economic, legal, as well as political reasons. At present, there appears to be a broad consensus that significant further institutional development of the EMS would require a major political initiative and necessitate an amendment of the Treaty that established the European Economic Community. Recent efforts to modify the operational procedures of the EMS and to increase its efficiency resulted in some changes but did not affect its basic institutional structure.

While the hopes of the optimists have been realized only in part, after more than seven years of EMS existence it has nevertheless become clear that the fears and predictions of the skeptics have not been justified. The widespread expectations that a system of fixed, though adjustable, exchange rates would not hold together for long or, conversely, that it would degenerate into a system of frequent small exchange rate adjustments, akin to a crawling peg, have not materialized. The countries participating in the exchange rate mechanism (ERM) of the EMS[2] have shown political determination to keep the system in operation. On a practical level, the participating central banks have demonstrated an unprecedented ability to work together in securing a smooth functioning of the system.

After some disappointing developments, in more recent years economic policies in the EMS countries have been increasingly oriented toward domestic stability and thus have facilitated a growing convergence in prices, costs, and monetary aggregates. While it may be debated whether the EMS and its constraints have been the main cause for this convergence, there is a consensus that the existence of the system has encouraged and contributed to the convergence of economic policies and developments. At the same time, the exchange rate variability of currencies participating in the ERM has significantly diminished since the establishment of the EMS, compared with earlier years and with other major currencies.

Other issues on the initial agenda have not been achieved: the United Kingdom is still not participating in the exchange rate mechanism, and Italy continues to avail itself of the wider fluctuation margins of 6 percent (compared with 2.25 percent for all other participants) that was intended as a transitory arrangement. By the same token, Greece, which joined the EC on January 1, 1981 and signed the EMS agreement in June 1985, is not a participant in the exchange rate mechanism. Spain and Portugal, members of the EC since January 1, 1986, are not yet participating in any aspect of the EMS.

From the outset, the EMS has shown considerable flexibility. The provisions that constitute the basis for its operation, as laid down in the Resolution of the European Council of December 5, 1978 and the Agreement between the EC central banks on the EMS of March 13, 1979,[3] serve only as a framework and do not prescribe the actual operation of the system in detail. Over time, the EMS has shown a gradual evolution in the role of the ECU (European Currency Unit), intervention policies, financing, the significance

---

[1] Commission of the European Communities, "The European Monetary System—Commentary, Documents," *European Economy* (Brussels), No. 3 (July 1979), pp. 95–97.

[2] At present, Belgium-Luxembourg, Denmark, France, the Federal Republic of Germany, Ireland, Italy, and the Netherlands participate in the exchange rate mechanism. Throughout this paper the term ERM is used to indicate these countries or their currencies. The term EMS is used in more general contexts.

[3] Henceforth called EMS Agreement. See: Committee of Governors of the Central Banks of the Member States of the European Economic Community and European Monetary Cooperation Fund, *Texts Concerning the European Monetary System,* 1985.

of the divergence indicator, and in other areas. In many ways, this gradual evolution was a response to emerging problems and needs but points also to changing philosophies and strategies of the participating central banks. Some of these changes are at variance with the hopes and views of some advocates of European integration who consider the system insufficiently oriented toward promotion of European integration through institutional arrangements and commitments and toward the goal of the European economic and monetary union. Another view is that too hasty a pace would only endanger what has been achieved so far.

From its inception in March 1979 through March 1983, the EMS experienced seven exchange rate realignments, which over time became more significant because of the size of the exchange rate adjustments and the number of currencies affected. During this period, the central rates of the deutsche mark rose cumulatively by about 33 percent against the French franc and by about 27 percent against the Belgian franc. The realignment of March 1983—the most comprehensive so far—was followed by a long period without changes in central rates until July 1985, when the Italian lira was devalued relative to the other currencies participating in the exchange rate mechanism. These two years and four months represent the longest period of exchange rate stability under the EMS or its predecessor, the European Common Margins Arrangement ("snake"). Several factors have contributed to this development: the growing convergence of economic performance among EMS countries, the increased credibility of the system as a result of the commitment of the participating central banks to the maintenance of stable exchange rates, and developments in international exchange markets, in particular the strength of the U.S. dollar during this period.

The dollar's strength reflected substantial capital flows to the United States, which at times exerted a downward pressure on the deutsche mark exchange rate vis-à-vis its partner currencies in the ERM.

Following the French parliamentary elections in March 1986, a general realignment of exchange rates, initiated by the French authorities, took place in April 1986, in which the French franc was devalued by about 6 percent against the deutsche mark and the Netherlands guilder, roughly offsetting the accumulated differences in unit labor cost increases between France and the Federal Republic of Germany; the other currencies were devalued by roughly 2 to 3 percent against the deutsche mark and the Netherlands guilder. Four months later, in August 1986, the Irish pound was devalued relative to the other participating currencies.

The present paper provides a survey of recent developments in the EMS.[4] In Section II, the paper discusses membership in the EMS and changes in the operation and in the institutional design of the system. In the next section, exchange rate developments over the last few years are summarized. Section IV analyzes the variability of exchange rates in the EMS over the period 1979–85 and compares it with earlier periods and with the experience outside the EMS. The final section of the paper focuses on convergence of economic developments between EMS countries and provides a comparison with other countries. Statistical information, legal texts concerning the EMS, and a short, selective bibliography are contained in appendices.

---

[4] It complements and updates an earlier paper by Horst Ungerer, Owen Evans, and Peter Nyberg on EMS developments: *The European Monetary System: The Experience, 1979–1982*, Occasional Paper No. 19 (Washington: International Monetary Fund, 1983). Hereafter referred to as Ungerer (1983).

II The System and Its Development

This section summarizes the main characteristics and operational elements of the EMS, as laid down in the EMS Agreement, and surveys their evolution in the context of the actual operation of the EMS by the participating central banks over the last few years. The section also discusses efforts to adapt the written rules governing the system to changing needs and to the emerging actual management of the system, which resulted in an amendment of the EMS Agreement in June 1985.

Membership in the European Monetary System and Participation in the Exchange Rate Mechanism

The EMS came into operation on March 13, 1979 and the nine EC countries became members of the system when their central banks signed the EMS Agreement. All EC countries but the United Kingdom decided to become participants in the exchange rate mechanism of the EMS, thus accepting the related obligations. The pound sterling, however, was from the beginning part of the basket of currencies forming the ECU. On July 6, 1979, the United Kingdom followed the other EMS countries and deposited, on a voluntary basis, 20 percent of its gold and gross dollar assets with the European Monetary Cooperation Fund (EMCF)[5] in exchange for an equivalent amount of ECUs.

Greece became a member of the EC on January 1, 1981, but did not join the EMS. The EC Council of Ministers decided to include the Greek drachma in the ECU basket on September 17, 1984, when a general revision of the currency composition of the ECU was instituted. On June 10, 1985, Greece signed the EMS Agreement and deposited 20 percent of its gold and gross dollar reserves in exchange for ECUs on Jan-

uary 1, 1986, but did not become a participant in the exchange rate mechanism of the EMS. On January 1, 1986 Spain and Portugal became members of the EC, bringing total membership to 12. Neither joined the EMS but Spain indicated its interest in membership in due course. It was agreed that the Spanish peseta and the Portuguese escudo could be included in the ECU on the occasion of the next regular review of the ECU basket scheduled for 1989. In the case of Greece as well as Portugal and Spain, the main reasons for not joining the EMS or for not becoming a participant in the exchange rate mechanism for the time being were the substantial structural differences between their economies and those of the other EC members, in particular the highly industrial countries, and the need to allow their economies time to adjust gradually to membership in the EC without excessive constraints.

More significant for the actual functioning of the EMS as well as its international importance and weight is the fact that the United Kingdom is still not participating in the exchange rate mechanism. This means that the pound sterling continues to float independently and that U.K. exchange rate and monetary policies are not subject to the constraints of a fixed-exchange rate system and, by the same token, do not benefit from any advantages the ERM may confer on participants, such as lower exchange rate variability.

Ever since the establishment of the EMS, on economic as well as on political grounds there have been calls for participation of the United Kingdom in all its activities. These calls have come from EC partner countries, the EC Commission, and from within the United Kingdom. British businessmen and academicians have taken the view that U.K. participation in the exchange rate mechanism would on the whole be beneficial. The question has been discussed at several occasions in both houses of Parliament[6] but, in the end, the U.K. authorities have always concluded that the time was not yet ripe for full membership.

The main arguments against full membership of the

---

[5] The EMCF was established as an institution of the EC in April 1973 and has served as the administrator for transactions under the European Common Margins Arrangement and the EMS as well as the very short-term financing facility and facility for short-term monetary support.

[6] See, for example, Treasury and Civil Service Committee, House of Commons, various documents from Sessions 1981–82, 1982–83, and 1984–85.

United Kingdom can be summarized as follows.[7] The pound sterling is subject to external influences that differ substantially from those of other EC currencies, as is illustrated by the wide fluctuations in the sterling/deutsche mark exchange rate. Two factors account for this phenomenon. First, there is the "petrocurrency effect" attributable to the United Kingdom's role as a large net exporter of oil. Second, the pound and the deutsche mark have often behaved differently at times of large swings in the external value of the dollar. Since the pound is an important trading currency, and exchange controls have been abolished, the volume of intervention necessary to defend the pound in case of a sustained attack could be much larger than that necessary for most other EC currencies. A large volume of intervention could, in turn, jeopardize domestic monetary objectives. For those reasons, it is argued, ERM participation "would involve in unfavorable circumstances greater interest rate volatility and perhaps more frequent realignments than many of its advocates admit."[8]

The advocates of ERM participation have maintained that the petrocurrency argument is becoming less important over time, that monetary targeting has already become less prominent in the United Kingdom's economic strategy and the exchange rate is receiving increasing importance in the conduct of monetary policy, and that there is now a high degree of economic convergence between the United Kingdom and the Federal Republic of Germany, the most important economy among the present ERM participants, a convergence that would facilitate U.K. participation. Past experience with exchange rate variability could not be considered a guide for the future since economic convergence, ERM participation with the inherent commitment to a fixed exchange rate, and a monetary policy consistent with a system of fixed exchange rates would positively influence exchange rate expectations and thus lower exchange rate variability.[9]

Evolution of the System

Exchange Rate and Intervention Mechanism

The central element of the EMS is a system of fixed but adjustable exchange rates in which each participating currency is tied to each of the other participating currencies by bilateral central rates. Around the bilateral central rates, fluctuation margins of 2.25 percent (6 percent in the case of the Italian lira) have been established that determine the bilateral intervention points for each currency against each of the other currencies. At these points, intervention in the partner currency concerned is obligatory and potentially unlimited in amount. The necessary funds for carrying out such intervention are supplied by the respective partner central banks under mutual credit lines (the "very short-term financing facility"). Claims and debts stemming from obligatory intervention are settled subject to provisions laid down in the EMS Agreement. These rules are not, however, rigid and narrow; rather they provide an overall framework for and leave substantial flexibility in the timing and means of settlement. With little exaggeration, the provisions of the agreement could be characterized as a fall-back mechanism of obligations that comes into play to the extent that the partners do not agree on other ways to settle their mutual claims and debts. An important element in the initial settlement rules is that a debtor is entitled to use ECUs up to 50 percent of the amount due; use of ECUs beyond that point is subject to an agreement with the creditor.[10]

The grid of bilateral rates is supplemented by the "divergence indicator" that shows the movements of

---

[7] A. Loehnis, "The EMS: A Central Banking Perspective," speech given at the Federal Trust Conference "The Time is Ripe" on June 19, 1985; in *Auszüge aus Presseartikeln*, Deutsche Bundesbank (Frankfurt), July 3, 1985.

[8] Loehnis, *ibid.* Recently, A. Walters argued against U.K. participation in the ERM by criticizing the EMS for suffering from an inherent contradiction: as long as inflation rates differ, a fixed exchange rate system will lead to rather perverse monetary policies. Thus, if the rates of inflation are 15 percent in Italy and 3 percent in the Federal Republic of Germany, with freely mobile capital and fixed exchange rates between the two countries, nominal interest rates have to be the same, say 9 percent. This leads to real interest rates of plus 6 percent in Germany and minus 6 percent in Italy. If monetary authorities operate an interest-rate regime in controlling their domestic money supply, there will be great pressure to expand money and credit in Italy, whereas in Germany there will be a substantial financial squeeze. This was precisely the opposite monetary policy to that which would move toward convergence (A. Walters, *Britain's Economic Renaissance* (New York: Oxford University, 1986), pp. 126–127). Walters' argument is, however, based on the somewhat unrealistic premise that such a wide differential in inflation rates would not be reflected in expectations of frequent and large realignments of exchange rates. For a response to Walters' argumentation, see M. Russo, "Why the Time is Ripe," lecture delivered to the Bow Group, House of Commons; London, May 19, 1986.

[9] For views in favor of U.K. participation, see e.g.: Federal Trust for Education and Research, "The Time is Ripe—The European Monetary System, the ECU, and British Policy," Dr. David Lomax, Rapporteur, November 1984; A. Scott, "Britain and the EMS: An Appraisal of the Report of the Treasury and Civil Service Committee," *Journal of Common Market Studies* (Oxford), Vol. XXIV, No. 3 (March 1986), pp. 188–201; Public Policy Centre, *The Need for an Exchange Rate Policy and the Option of Full U.K. Membership in the EMS*, Unpublished manuscript, London, May 1986; M. Russo, *ibid.*

[10] Additionally, the amendment of the EMS Agreement of June 1985 provides the possibility of mobilizing ECU holdings to obtain intervention currencies. See below.

the exchange rate of each participating currency against the (weighted) average movement of the other participating currencies. The underlying idea is that the indicator would induce changes of policies at an early stage and thus help to keep exchange rates within the margins. Areas for possible immediate action include domestic monetary policy and intramarginal intervention including the use of third currencies, such as the U.S. dollar. While at times movements of the divergence indicator have resulted in some action, the indicator has never been fully able, as its proponents had hoped, to assume the role of linking exchange rate developments to an increasing convergence of economic policy, for example, by triggering restrictive measures in the case of a weak currency or expansionary measures in the case of a strong currency.[11]

Over the years, a marked shift in views has taken place regarding the relative merits of exchange rate flexibility and stability within the margins vis-à-vis other participating currencies. On the one hand, the flexibility provided by the fluctuation margins was regarded as a cushion to absorb or dampen some external shocks without the need for immediate changes in basic policies or central rates. Full use of the fluctuation margins would also help to limit exchange market intervention and thus avoid some of its potentially undesirable consequences. On the other hand, there are arguments in favor of keeping the exchange rate stable against other, particularly strong currencies in the system, if need be by intervening and by shifting interest rate differentials. By doing so, the authorities hope to influence market sentiments and exchange rate expectations by showing determination and by preventing the building up of a momentum for exchange rate movements. A related argument is that domestic monetary stability, in terms of actual developments and expectations, may be better served by exchange rate stability against key participating currencies.

Over time, the latter view has gained favor, and a number of EMS central banks have adopted a strategy of keeping their exchange rates well within the band of the EMS and minimizing movements against key currencies of the EMS. At times, this has required substantial intervention in the foreign exchange market and the maintenance of higher interest rates than might have been desirable from the point of view of domestic policy. In this way, the countries concerned not only strengthened the confidence of the market in their own policies and the exchange rate of their currency but also contributed to a greater convergence toward domestic cost and price stability within the EMS.

Thus, domestic policies of these countries have become more compatible with their exchange rate objectives.

Technically, this shift in strategy implied increased intramarginal intervention by central banks in place of intervention at the margins. While in the early years of the EMS obligatory intervention at the margins accounted for a substantial part of total intervention, more recently most intervention has been within the margins, and this has had significant repercussions for the functioning of the EMS. As a consequence, the very short-term financing facility that applies only to obligatory intervention at the margins in participating currencies has recently been rarely used, and the role of the ECU in financing intervention has been substantially reduced. In a temporary reversal of this trend, after the realignment of April 7, 1986, there was heavy intervention at the margins in support of the deutsche mark, which had moved from its position at the top of the band, prior to the realignment, to the bottom. A small part of these interventions was settled by the Bundesbank in ECUs, resulting in liabilities of the Bundesbank to the EMCF at the end of May 1986.[12]

According to Article 15 of the EMS Agreement, participating central banks are entitled to hold only working balances in other participating currencies, and these limits can only be exceeded with the consent of the central bank concerned. This provision, however, has been applied flexibly. In particular, the Deutsche Bundesbank, the issuer of the main EMS intervention currency, has consented to other central banks holding substantial amounts of deutsche mark and, on occasion, has encouraged them to acquire deutsche mark when market conditions made this appropriate. Any use of partner currencies for intramarginal intervention has remained, however, subject to approval by the issuing central bank. During periods of strength of its currency, the Deutsche Bundesbank has at times been reluctant to see larger injections of its currency into the market as this may have been in conflict with its own domestic monetary targets. Furthermore, other central banks have felt that obtaining approval for the use of a partner currency for intervention purposes provided insufficient flexibility for timely and efficient action. Since similar limitations and considerations did not apply to intervention in U.S. dollars, the latter has become an important intervention currency within the EMS.[13]

With a view to facilitating intramarginal intervention

---

[11] Some of the reasons for this development have been discussed in Ungerer (1983), p.15.

[12] See Deutsche Bundesbank, *Monthly Report* (Frankfurt), June 1986, p. 44.

[13] More recently, for similar reasons, some EMS central banks have also used previously acquired assets in private ECUs for intervention purposes.

in EMS currencies, various proposals for rule changes have been advanced. One has been to make the automatic provision of EMS currencies for obligatory intervention under the very short-term financing facility also available for intramarginal intervention. Another proposal has been to enable central banks in need of intervention currencies to obtain them against ECUs from other participating central banks.

After long discussions in the various competent bodies of the EC, the Monetary Committee and the Committee of the Governors of the Central Banks, as well as by the Finance Ministers, a package of amendments to the EMS Agreement was adopted in June 1985, which allowed a limited possibility for the mobilization of ECUs for obtaining intervention currencies, together with other provisions designed to increase the attractiveness of the official ECU as a reserve asset; the amendments are described below.

Credit Facilities

Apart from the very short-term facility for the financing of obligatory intervention, other credit facilities exist, which are not, however, limited to participants in the exchange rate mechanism of the EMS but open to all EC member countries. The short-term monetary support (STMS) is a quasi-automatic short-term facility. The medium-term financial assistance (MTFA) and the Community loan mechanism are medium-term facilities, whose use is subject to conditionality. In contrast to the STMS and the MTFA, whose credits are financed by EC partner countries, the Community loan mechanism relies on outside borrowing.[14]

Following the general realignment of exchange rates within the EMS in March 1983, France requested a loan of ECU 4 billion[15] under the Community loan mechanism. In May 1983, the Council of Ministers agreed to the request on the basis of an adjustment program to which France had committed itself.[16] The program included a reduction of the public sector deficit and of the target for the growth of the money supply, encouragement of private savings, and continued efforts to eliminate indexation both of costs and prices. While not all the objectives of the French program were attained, the improvement in the balance of payments that subsequently occurred nonetheless allowed the French authorities to make advance repayments on its loan of US$650 million in August 1985 and of a further US$1.8 billion in July 1986; the bulk of the remainder had been refinanced on more favorable terms earlier in 1985.

In December 1985, the Council of Ministers granted Greece a loan of ECU 1,750 million[17] under the same facility.[18] The loan was tied to a two-year recovery program that had as its main objectives a slowdown in the inflation of prices and labor costs through a lasting adjustment of the wage indexation mechanism, a reduction in the public sector borrowing requirement and in domestic credit expansion, and a reduction in the current account deficit. The loan is being made in two equal installments, the second of which is to be released subject to a mid-term review of the economic recovery program in November 1986.

Comparison of these two loans under the Community loan mechanism and their conditionality suggests that the EC has opted for a case-by-case approach. The loan to France was made in one amount, while the loan to Greece is being made in two installments. The program initiated by the French authorities included quantitative targets for public sector deficits and the growth of money supply, while that for Greece defined quantitative targets for inflation, the public sector borrowing requirement, and domestic credit expansion. Both programs emphasize the elimination or modification of indexation mechanisms. For France, external balance is an overall objective; for Greece, the objective of reducing the current account deficit is linked to the stabilization of the external public debt.

---

[14] The STMS was established in 1970 and enlarged when the EMS was established and in connection with the enlargements of the EC in 1973, 1981, and 1986. The facility is administered by the central banks and provides short-term financing in case of a temporary balance of payments deficit or a sudden decline in foreign exchange reserves. Credits are not subject to specific conditionality. The STMS was used by Italy in 1974, but has not been used since the EMS came into operation. Credits and contributions under the STMS are limited by creditor and debtor quotas (see Table 1). The MTFA was set up in 1971 and, like the STMS, was enlarged on several occasions. It provides credits for a period of two to five years when an EC country is in balance of payments difficulties or is seriously threatened with such difficulties. The Council of Ministers determines the amount and the duration of a credit and decides the applicable economic policy conditions. The facility was used by Italy in 1975 but has not been activated since the establishment of the EMS. The MTFA has a system of credit ceilings; normally no member country may draw more than 50 percent of the total credit ceilings (see Table 1). The Community loan mechanism was established in 1975. Under this facility the EC, authorized by the Council of Ministers, borrows and on-lends to member countries amounts of up to ECU 8 billion (before 1985, ECU 6 billion). The Council

also determines the modalities and conditionality of any loan. Normally, any one member country may not borrow more than 50 percent of the total amount.

[15] Equivalent to US$3.7 billion at the then prevailing exchange rates.

[16] Council Decision (EEC) of May 16, 1983, *Official Journal of the European Communities*, No. L 153, June 11, 1983.

[17] Equivalent to US$1.6 billion at the then prevailing exchange rates.

[18] Council Decision (EEC) of December 9, 1985, *Official Journal of the European Communities*, No. L 341, December 12, 1985.

Role of the ECU

The ECU was introduced in connection with the establishment of the EMS. It was assigned three functions: first, as a means of settlement, second, (with a number of qualifications) as a reserve asset, and third, as a unit of account for financial transactions. In the latter capacity, the ECU serves not only as unit of account for various purposes in the EMS (central rates, reference point for the divergence indicator) or EMS-related institutions, such as the European Monetary Cooperation Fund or the various credit facilities, but also as the unit of account and value for all financial activities of the EC, such as the budget, the Common Agricultural Policy, the European Development Fund, and the European Investment Bank.

As a means of settlement and reserve asset, the ECU has not acquired the prominence its creators intended. As a means of settlement, use of the ECU has remained limited since the beginning. Net ECU holdings of central banks (representing the counterpart to the net use of ECUs) have never gone beyond 10 percent of the total amount of ECUs created through the swap arrangements with the EMCF; however, the use of ECUs by individual central banks has at times gone noticeably beyond 10 percent of their ECU holdings. As mentioned above, in the more recent past, the use of ECUs for settlement purposes has virtually ceased because of changes in intervention practices. It also should be noted that—contrary to the intentions expressed in the European Council Resolution of December 5, 1978—the EMS has not evolved "into a final system . . . [which] will entail the creation of the European Monetary Fund . . . as well as the full utilization of the ECU as a reserve asset and a means of settlement." This and the institutional limitations on the use of ECUs—it cannot be used directly for intervention and it can be used only within specified limits for the settlement of intervention debts within the EMS—make the ECU less than a full reserve asset. In essence, at present it is a substitute for those reserves (gold and U.S. dollar holdings) that have been deposited with the EMCF (Table 2).

In view of this situation, proposals have been put forward to expand the possibilities for use of the ECU as a means of settlement and to increase its attractiveness as a reserve asset. Other proposals have been aimed at a more rationally controlled process of creating ECUs. Under the present rules, the creation of ECUs is largely determined by variables outside the direct control of the EMS authorities.[19] The main proposals have been to improve the remuneration on net ECU holdings and to abolish the acceptance limit for its use in settlement of obligatory intervention debts. As already mentioned, there have also been suggestions to make the very short-term financing facility available for intramarginal intervention and thus to make ECUs eligible for the settlement of obligations stemming from this kind of intervention.[20]

Private ECUs[21]

The legal texts introducing and defining the ECU stipulate its use for official purposes. No provision is made for the use of ECUs in private transactions. The idea of the ECU as a basket of EC currencies was so appealing to financial markets, however, that soon after its introduction a private market for ECUs emerged and has expanded rapidly over recent years.

As the ECU is not officially issued to the public, that is, there are no coins or banknotes, the private ECU is essentially book money. Banks create it by crediting sums to an ECU account. Hence, the private ECU market is completely independent of official ECU creation and is not subject to national or supranational monetary control. There are, however, national regulations on the use of private ECUs.

At present, major financial instruments available for national currencies are also available for the ECU. Banks offer accounts for sight and time deposits in ECUs and participate in ECU bond issues. The whole spectrum of loans ranging from personal to major syndicated loans are available in ECUs, and, in 1984, floating rate notes and zero coupon issues were introduced. Also, an ECU credit card and traveller's checks denominated in ECUs are available. The relative success of the private ECU is the result of a number of favorable factors such as the attractive combination of reasonable yields and perceived low or modest risk associated with its exchange value in terms of EC currencies owing to the workings of the exchange rate mechanism of the EMS, the favorable treatment given to its use in the capital controls of some EC members, and the encouragement and support given to its development by EC institutions and some European governments and central banks.

---

[19] For details see Ungerer (1983), p. 16; see also Table 2.

[20] The changes regarding the use and the characteristics of the ECU finally adopted are described below.

[21] For a more comprehensive discussion of the private ECU see R.S. Masera, "An Increasing Role of the ECU: A Character in Search of a Script," Unpublished manuscript, Rome, April 1986; H.W. Mayer, "Private ECUs—Potential Macro-Economic Policy Discussions," *Economic Papers*, Bank for International Settlements (Basel), No. 16 (April 1986); International Monetary Fund, Treasurer's and Research Departments, "Role of the SDR in the International Monetary System," forthcoming Occasional Paper.

Changes in the Institutional Setup of the EMS

The EMS Agreement

Over the years the EMS has undergone a number of changes in its modes of operation. These occurred without modifications in the institutional setup of the EMS and remained within the framework laid down in the EMS Agreement, which has proved sufficiently flexible to accommodate these changes. According to one view, however, these changes constitute a move away from the original intentions for the role and ultimate purpose of the EMS. Accordingly, various proposals have been made for institutional changes and the further development of the system, dealing, among other matters, with the role and functions of a European Monetary Fund and the scope for coordinated intervention policies vis-à-vis third currencies. Because of the complex political, institutional, economic, and technical nature of the proposals, however, no final agreements could be reached.

The evolution of the system also brought to the surface a number of issues which, though more operational, were by no means only technical. After extensive discussions within the EC, the Committee of Governors of Central Banks adopted on June 10, 1985 the following package of amendments to the EMS Agreement intended to address these problems. The amendments became effective on July 1, 1985.[22]

a. Central banks with a need for intervention currencies may mobilize through the European Monetary Cooperation Fund their net creditor positions in ECUs together with part of those ECUs allocated to them by the EMCF (against the deposit of 20 percent of their gold and U.S. dollar holdings). EMS central banks have committed themselves to cover such mobilization operations by providing U.S. dollars within specified limits. The dollars thus provided may be exchanged for participating EMS currencies with the approval of the issuing central banks. Mobilization operations will run for three months, with the possibility of renewal for a further three-month period (Article 18a of the Agreement). This provision was used for the first time by a participating central bank at the end of 1985.

b. The payments ratio that limits settlements in official ECUs of obligations arising out of the use of very short-term financing will remain at 50 percent as a general rule, but this limit will be waived to the extent that the recipient central bank is itself a net debtor in ECUs (amended Article 16.1).

c. The interest rate on net positions in ECUs and of ECU-denominated claims under the very short-term financing facility (previously the weighted average of the official discount rates of the EC countries) will henceforth be based on the weighted average of representative money-market rates in those EC countries whose currencies make up the ECU basket (amended Article 8).

d. Central banks of nonmember countries and international monetary institutions, such as the Bank for International Settlements, may be accorded the status of "other holder" by the EMCF Board of Governors and thus enabled to obtain official ECUs from EMS central banks by means of sale and repurchase agreements or reversible swap transactions.

The latter change required a decision, taken in October 1985, by the EC Council of Ministers.[23] Subsequently, the EMCF Board took a decision laying down the terms and conditions for acquisition, holding and use of ECUs by "other holders." The Bank for International Settlements became the first other holder of ECUs on January 14, 1986.

Composition of the ECU

Like its predecessor, the EUA (European Unit of Account, introduced in 1975), the ECU was originally defined by fixed amounts of the currencies of the nine countries that in 1979 constituted the EC.

In establishing the ECU, provision was made for periodic re-examinations and revisions of its composition to take account of changes in member countries' economic situations and exchange rates.[24] The first re-examination and, if necessary, possible revision of the ECU basket was to be made within six months after the EMS entered into force and thereafter every five years or, on request, if the weight of any currency had

---

[22] Committee of Governors of the Central Banks of the Member States of the European Economic Community, Press Communiqué, June 10, 1985; see also S. Micossi, "The Intervention and Financing Mechanisms of the EMS and the Role of the ECU," *Quarterly Review*, Banca Nazionale del Lavoro (Rome), December 1985, pp. 405–24.

[23] Council Regulation (EEC) No. 3066/85 of October 28, 1985, *Official Journal of the European Communities*, No. L 290, November 1, 1985.

[24] According to the Resolution of the European Council of December 5, 1978 on the establishment of the EMS, revisions of the composition of the ECU have to be mutually accepted, must not by themselves modify the external value of the ECU (as expressed in any one currency), and must be made in line with underlying economic criteria. A revision requires a unanimous decision by the EC Council of Ministers, acting on a proposal from the EC Commission, after consultation with the Monetary Committee and the Board of Governors of the European Monetary Cooperation Fund.

changed by 25 percent or more.[25] The first re-examination took place in September 1979 and did not lead to any change in the ECU's composition. The next re-examination was therefore scheduled for September 1984.

A need for revision can also arise because of changes in the membership of the EC. When Greece joined the EC in January 1981, it was agreed that the drachma would be included in the ECU basket at the latest by December 31, 1985 or earlier if a revision of the basket took place in accordance with the above-mentioned provisions.

On September 15, 1984, when the regular re-examination was due, the EC Council of Ministers decided to change the currency composition of the ECU and, at the request of the Greek government, to include the drachma in the basket. The decision came into force on September 17, 1984.[26] According to the declaration of the Council, the revision was carried out "taking into account the underlying economic criteria, as well as the need to ensure the smooth functioning of the market." Table 4 shows the amounts of the currencies defining the ECU and their percentage weights on March 13, 1979, when the EMS started operations, and on September 17, 1984.

The revision largely offset the effects of past realignments of exchange rates in the EMS on the percentage weights of the currencies in the ECU basket and brought them more in line with the relative economic importance of EC countries. The percentage weights of September 17, 1984, however, were different from what they were initially in 1975, when the basket was established to define the EUA (see Tables 3 and 4). Compared with March 1979, the weights of the pound sterling, the Italian lira and the Irish pound were allowed to increase. Furthermore, the Greek drachma was included in the ECU with an amount equivalent to 1.3 percent. In comparison with the percentage weights based on market exchange rates prior to the revision, on September 14, 1984, the weights, especially of the deutsche mark and the Netherlands guilder, were lowered while those of the French franc and the Italian lira were raised.

While the revision of the ECU basket changed the amount of each national currency in the basket, it left the external value of the ECU (the value of the ECU expressed in any one currency) unaffected at the time

of transition.[27] The revision did not cause any change in the ECU central rates of participating currencies nor in the grid of bilateral central rates and bilateral intervention limits.

Future Development of the EMS

There seems to be now a broad consensus within the EC that on the basis of the existing legal framework, the EMS cannot be substantially changed or further developed. Moreover, several countries have argued that changes in the system as operated now, such as the participation of the United Kingdom in the exchange rate mechanism and the narrowing of the fluctuation band for the Italian lira as well as the liberalization of capital movements in the EC, were prerequisites for a further significant development. Some countries still see scope for more action, but others feel that such action would not be desirable and could undermine the basic objective of the EMS, which is to establish a "zone of monetary stability in Europe," as long as a high degree of economic convergence was still lacking. While there is now a general agreement that the system has been quite successful in providing a high degree of exchange rate stability and in fostering economic convergence, views differ as to whether or not further efforts in the immediate future to develop the system would strengthen it and promote European economic integration.

This difference in views goes back to the first major political effort in 1969 to complement the provisions of the EEC Treaty (which basically provided for a customs union with common policies in such areas as foreign trade and agriculture) by establishing an economic and monetary union within a decade. This resulted in the Werner Plan (named after Pierre Werner, then Prime Minister of Luxembourg and Chairman of a specially appointed committee).[28] The European Common Margins Arrangement—in certain respects a predecessor of the EMS—was the only significant result. A heated debate, not limited to official circles, ensued about the best way to achieve progress. One prevalent opinion was that major progress toward institutionalized forms of monetary integration, involving fixed exchange rates and leading ultimately to a common currency, would first require a high degree of coordination of economic policies, based on a firm

---

[25] The percentage weight of currency i in the ECU basket is given by $w(i) = z(i)/x(i)$ where $w(i)$ is the percentage weight of currency i, $z(i)$ is the number of units of currency i in the ECU basket, and $x(i)$ is the external value of the ECU in terms of currency i. Thus, if currency i appreciates (depreciates) against the ECU, its percentage weight in the basket increases (decreases).

[26] Council Regulation (EEC) No. 2626/84 of September 15, 1984, *Official Journal of the European Communities*, No. L 247, September 26, 1984.

[27] The value of the ECU in terms of currency i is given by $x(i) = z(i)/w(i)$ where symbols have the same denotation as in footnote 25. Thus, the value of the ECU in terms, say, of the deutsche mark was given on September 14, 1984 by 0.828 DM/0.369 = 2.25 DM and on September 17, 1984 by 0.719 DM/0.32 = 2.25 DM.

[28] See *Official Journal of the European Communities*, No. C 136/1, November 11, 1970.

political commitment. In short, a common European currency could only be the crowning achievement of the process of economic integration. The other, equally eloquently defended viewpoint was that economic and monetary integration required a strong institutional framework, which in turn would induce and promote the needed economic policy cooperation. These two basic philosophies[29] are still at the heart of the debate about the pace and scope for monetary integration in the EC, although it is now increasingly recognized that there exists an interdependence between building institutions and achieving greater economic cooperation and, consequently, convergence in economic performance.

The view now prevails that any move toward a "second phase" of the EMS (initially envisaged two years after its coming into existence) would require a major political initiative. Such a phase would not be possible on the basis of the EEC Treaty and of existing agreements, but rather would require a new legal framework, that is, an amendment of the EEC Treaty to be ratified by national parliaments and substantial consequent national legislation. This holds in particular for such issues as a permanent pooling of reserves, the authority for the EMCF (or a future European Monetary Fund) to issue ECUs against national currency or "ex nihilo," and for empowering the EMCF to intervene directly in the exchange markets.

In June 1985, the European Council, composed of the Heads of State and Government of the EC countries, agreed at a meeting in Milan to convene an intergovernmental conference to study the implementation of institutional changes and an extension of the Community's activities with a view to amending the EEC Treaty accordingly. An agreement on those issues was reached by the European Council at its meeting in Luxembourg in December 1985. The reform package (Single European Act) was officially signed by representatives of the EC member countries in February 1986.[30] It is now subject to parliamentary procedures according to national laws. The intended amendments to the EEC Treaty include, among a broad range of other issues, the insertion of a new Article 102 A in Title II "Economic Policy" of the Treaty addressing cooperation in economic and monetary policy. The Article would make explicit reference to the EMS and the ECU and refer also to Article 236 of the EEC Treaty "insofar as further development in the field of economic and monetary policy necessitates institutional changes." Article 236 deals with the amendment of the EEC Treaty (see Appendix II). This particular proposed amendment is seen as anchoring the principle of monetary cooperation as well as the need for a convergence of economic and monetary policies firmly in the EEC Treaty while at the same time acknowledging that substantial institutional changes must take the form of an amendment of the Treaty.

In the wake of these events, in June 1986, the EC Commission proposed a specific timetable for the progressive liberalization of capital movements within the EC with a view to furthering convergence of economic policies within the EMS.[31] In a first step, capital transactions most directly involved in the functioning of the Common Market must be freed in 1986; in a second step, all remaining capital transactions would be liberalized by 1992. In addition, restrictions that are maintained by EC member countries under safeguard clauses in case of balance of payments difficulties would require special derogations. The initiatives for a further liberalization of capital movements within the EC have triggered a debate about the consequences it might have on the functioning and cohesion of the EMS. One view is that, given existing divergences in economic performance, in particular with regard to inflation and interest rates, any significant progress toward free mobility of capital would facilitate large scale destabilizing capital movements frustrating efforts to maintain exchange rate stability. Another view is that the liberalization of capital movements would intensify pressure on EMS countries to adopt compatible economic policies leading to convergent economic developments.

---

[29] To distinguish those two schools of thought by the terms "économistes" and "monétaristes" makes some sense in French or German but not in English.

[30] For the text of the "Single European Act" see *Bulletin of the European Communities*, Supplement 2/86.

[31] For details see Commission of the European Communities, *Communication to the Council: Programme for Liberalization of Capital Movements in the Community* (Brussels: Commission of the European Communities, 1986).

III Exchange Rate Developments

Overview

From its inception until 1983 the EMS was characterized by frequent periods of exchange market strain and numerous consequent realignments of central rates among currencies participating in the ERM (Tables 5–10). Realignments took place in September and November 1979, March and October 1981, February and June 1982, and March 1983. The general experience in these periods of strain suggested that resisting market pressure through intervention and short-term monetary measures could buy time for a weak currency by redirecting capital flows in favor of countries with high nominal interest rates, but that in the absence of appropriate and sufficient policy measures aimed at the underlying causes of weakness, exchange rate changes would eventually become inevitable. In these early years, the size and frequency of central rate realignments increased significantly, indicating that the needed drive for greater economic convergence to generate stable exchange rates had achieved only limited success (Chart 1).[32]

Since 1983, however, convergence of economic policies and developments among EMS countries have laid the groundwork for greater exchange rate stability (see Section V). Nevertheless, exchange rate developments in the EMS during the two years to mid-1985 also have to be seen in the light of the strong and rising dollar, which was in turn influenced by the mix of financial policies in the United States that led to high nominal and real U.S. interest rates, both in absolute terms and relative to other countries. The value of the ECU in terms of dollars, which had been as high as US$1.44 at the end of 1979, had fallen to a little less than a dollar per ECU by the turn of 1982. With occasional mild interruptions the ECU continued to fall throughout 1983 and 1984 and the first two months of 1985, reaching a nadir of US$0.67 in February 1985. Subsequently, the dollar weakened and the dollar value of the ECU rose to US$0.83 by September

1985.[33] Since the Group of Five meeting in New York on September 22, 1985 and the announced intention of major countries to reduce the value of the dollar against other currencies, the EMS currencies have further strengthened against the dollar, reflecting the effect of both intervention by Group of Five central banks and narrowed interest differentials. By October 1986, the value of the ECU had advanced to US$1.04.

Experience shows that periods of weakness of the dollar tend to coincide with increased tension in the EMS, since at such times capital appears to move disproportionately from dollars into deutsche mark.[34] Explanations offered include the limited role played by EMS currencies other than the deutsche mark as alternative reserve and investment currencies, along with the general perception of Germany as a low inflation country. By contrast, a strong dollar has in the past often been coincident with a lack of tension in the system. Against the background of this experience, it came as a surprise that the weakening of the dollar initially created only limited tension within the EMS. When it became clear, however, that the period of strength of the dollar was over, difficulties began to reemerge.

Exchange Rate Developments in the EMS Since 1983

In early 1983, there was widespread speculation of a possible realignment, directed particularly against the Belgian and French currencies. Significant intervention was required by several central banks to support these currencies. Speculative activity increased after parliamentary elections in Germany and municipal elections in France in March, necessitating further intervention in support of the French and

---

[32] For more details see Ungerer (1983), pp. 5–7.

[33] Figures for the U.S. dollar value of the ECU are monthly averages.

[34] M. Sarcinelli for example attributes a great weight to the dollar in explaining developments in the EMS. See M. Sarcinelli, "The EMS and the International Monetary System: Toward Greater Stability," *Quarterly Review*, Banca Nazionale del Lavoro (Rome), March 1986, pp. 57–83.

Chart 1. Movement of EMS Currency Exchange Rates Against the ECU

(Monthly averages, July 1979 = 100)

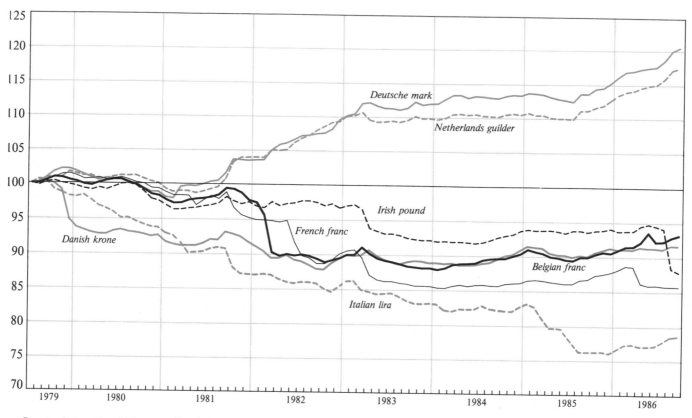

Source: International Monetary Fund, *International Financial Statistics*, various issues.

Belgian francs and the Italian lira. The Belgian, Danish, and Irish central banks raised key interest rates, and in France short-term interest rates were encouraged to rise substantially. Belgium announced emergency exchange controls. Over the weekend March 19–20 official discussions took place, but agreement was not reached and a realignment was effectively kept in abeyance.

On Monday, March 21, many European central banks suspended trading. Announcement of the agreed realignment was made in the afternoon of March 21 in Europe and became effective on March 22. The deutsche mark was revalued by 5.5 percent, the Netherlands guilder by 3.5 percent, the Danish krone by 2.5 percent, and the Belgian and Luxembourg francs by 1.5 percent, while the French and Italian currencies were devalued by 2.5 percent and the Irish pound by 3.5 percent. Like previous realignments, this realignment had become necessary as a result of the continued differences in the underlying strength of the participating countries' external positions, which reflected in turn divergences in economic policies and cost-price performance. These differences had generated expec-

tations of exchange rate changes and led to large speculative capital flows.

After the realignment, and as the result of a reversal of earlier capital flows, the deutsche mark and the Netherlands guilder moved to the bottom of the parity grid, while the French franc, the Irish pound and the Danish krone went to the top, with the Belgian franc in the middle. Interest rates returned to more normal levels, and suspicions that the French devaluation might have been too small subsided after the French authorities announced a program of restrictive financial measures.

From the March 1983 realignment until February 1985, the U.S. dollar gradually appreciated relative to European currencies, and the EMS experienced a period of relative internal stability. In spite of favorable current account and price developments in Germany, the deutsche mark did not come under upward pressure within the EMS largely because of strong capital flows to the United States. The exchange rates of other participants did not fall under pressure either, in spite of considerable, though reduced, divergences in cost and price performance among EMS countries.

After reaching a peak of DM 3.47 per US$1 on February 26, 1985, the U.S. dollar has been depreciating vis-à-vis the European currencies (Chart 2). The gradual depreciation of the dollar did not significantly affect the relative position of currencies within the EMS band in the first half of 1985: the Danish krone and the Irish pound remained in the upper half of the narrow band, while the Netherlands guilder and the deutsche mark remained in the lower half (Chart 3). The French franc, however, appreciated gradually and moved into the upper half of the narrow band in the second quarter of 1985, while the Italian lira, which had been in the upper half of the wide band in January–February 1985, moved to the lower part in March and remained there until July (Chart 4).

The performance of the Italian economy deteriorated in the first half of 1985, especially in the fiscal and

Chart 2.   Movements of the ECU Against the U.S. Dollar

(U.S. dollar per ECU, monthly averages)

Source: International Monetary Fund, *International Financial Statistics*, various issues.

external accounts. The worsening of the current account reflected primarily the maintenance of a rate of growth in domestic demand higher than that of Italy's partners as well as the lagged effects of a significant loss of competitiveness vis-à-vis other EMS countries over the previous two years. To halt the deterioration of the external position, in July 1985 the Italian authorities called for a realignment of exchange rates within the EMS. Effective July 22, the lira was devalued by 6 percent, and the other participating currencies revalued by 2 percent, implying a devaluation of the lira by 7.8 percent in terms of foreign currency per lira.

The July 22 realignment was not preceded by severe pressure on the exchange rate of the lira or on reserves, except on July 19, 1985, when, with the Bank of Italy abstaining from intervention in anticipation of a realignment over the weekend, a thin market was temporarily upset by a sizeable transaction; at this point, the authorities decided to close the market early. Following the realignment, the Italian lira was kept in the upper half of the wide band until April 1986.

Toward the end of July and in early August 1985, there was some speculation of a further realignment involving the French and Belgian francs. This speculation pushed up forward discounts of those two currencies, and the respective central banks intervened to support their currencies. After these periods of tension, the French franc continued its upward movement in the band, but the Belgian franc remained at the bottom of the narrow band, though well within the permitted range, reflecting the continuing policy of intramarginal intervention. In contrast to developments after previous, general realignments, the deutsche mark and the Netherlands guilder moved to the upper part of the narrow band in August.

The exchange market reaction to the Group of Five communiqué of September 22, 1985 was swift. The EMS currencies appreciated by 6 percent against the U.S. dollar on September 23 and by a further ½ percent the following day. By the end of September, the joint float had appreciated by 7½ to 8 percent against the dollar compared with the rate on September 20. The continuous downward movement of the dollar did not affect the relative position of EMS currencies until about December 1985, when foreign exchange market participants apparently became convinced of the determination of Group of Five central banks to lower the dollar and also began to take account of the improved growth prospects for Europe, in particular for Germany. As was the case before when the U.S. dollar depreciated, the deutsche mark, together with the Netherlands guilder, moved sharply upward in the narrow band, and the currencies of the smaller EMS members, such as the Danish krone and the Irish

Chart 3.   EMS: Position in the Narrow Band[1]

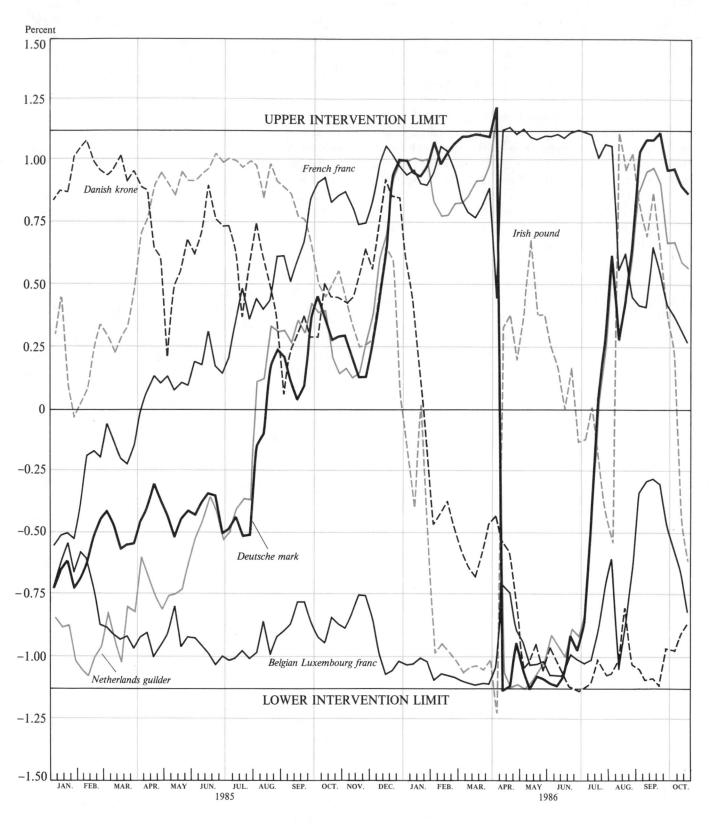

Sources: International Monetary Fund, *International Financial Statistics*, various issues; and Fund staff estimates.

[1]Weekly averages; Italian lira not included. The chart measures deviations of currencies from their bilateral central rates in terms of logarithmic differences between spot exchange rates and bilateral central rates multiplied by 100.

Chart 4. EMS: Position in the Wide Band[1]

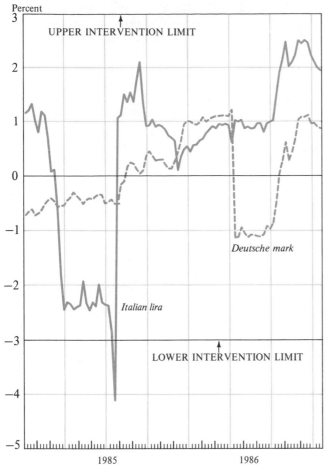

Sources: International Monetary Fund, *International Financial Statistics*, various issues; and Fund staff estimates.

[1] Weekly averages. The chart measures deviations of currencies from their bilateral central rates in terms of logarithmic differences between spot exchange rates and bilateral central rates multiplied by 100.

pound, weakened. While the Belgian franc remained in the lower part of the narrow band, the French franc remained strong, reflecting the improvement of the external position of the French economy, increased confidence in the anti-inflationary policies of the French Government, and the expectation that no realignment would take place until after the parliamentary elections in France in March 1986.

During the last few weeks of 1985 and in early 1986, the Belgian franc, the Irish pound, and the Italian lira came under renewed downward pressure. To defend the franc, which had been at the bottom of the narrow band since March 1985, the Belgian National Bank increased interest rates in December 1985 and intervened in foreign exchange markets. The Italian authorities tightened monetary policy and reinstated certain previously abolished foreign exchange control

measures in January 1986 to ease pressure on the lira. To stem the private capital outflow and relieve pressure against the Irish pound, the Central Bank of Ireland in the course of the first quarter of 1986 raised the interest rate at which it provides short-term support to the money market. As a result of these measures, as well as continuing intramarginal intervention, the Belgian franc and the Irish pound remained above the lower intervention limit, while the lira remained in the upper half of the wide band throughout the first quarter of 1986.

Exchange markets were generally calm during the remainder of the first quarter of 1986. The French franc weakened somewhat but remained in the upper half of the narrow band, while the Belgian franc and the Irish pound alternated at the bottom of the band. The Danish krone stabilized somewhat below its central rate, but well above the lower intervention limit. The deutsche mark and the Netherlands guilder were at the top of the band. The Italian lira, too, remained in the upper part of the wide band. Following the French elections on March 16, it appeared that markets considered an early exchange rate realignment and a devaluation of the French franc less likely, as the three-month forward discount of the franc fell from an average of 6 percent a year during the week before the elections to 4 percent a year in the week thereafter.

On Friday, April 4, 1986, EMS central banks suspended their official currency dealings after the Banque de France had informed them that it would not continue to support the franc. This created considerable movement in foreign exchange markets and caused the French franc and the Irish pound to fall below their (suspended) lower intervention limits, while the deutsche mark and the Netherlands guilder rose above their (suspended) upper intervention limits. Trading was thin on that day and the spread between buying and selling rates widened sharply. On April 6, 1986 the Ministers of Finance and Economics and the Central Bank Governors of the EC member countries decided on an adjustment of central rates within the EMS, which became effective on the following day. The deutsche mark and the Netherlands guilder were revalued by 3 percent, the Belgium/Luxembourg franc and the Danish krone were revalued by 1 percent, while the French franc was devalued by 3 percent. The Irish pound and the Italian lira did not move.

The realignment took place at the initiative of the French authorities, who sought a devaluation of the French franc as part of a package of measures designed to liberalize the French economy and strengthen its competitiveness. In support of the exchange rate adjustment, the French authorities took steps to slow nominal wage growth and to reduce the budget deficit and announced their objective of eliminating the noninterest component of the central government deficit in the course of the next three years. The target of containing the growth of M3 below 5 percent throughout the year was reasserted, and the authorities indicated their intention to support this target with a prudent interest rate policy, even though it implied continued relatively high real interest rates. Exchange controls were to be further relaxed, especially for business transactions, and the remaining price controls on industrial products were to be abolished.

When foreign exchange markets reopened after the realignment, the deutsche mark and the Netherlands guilder moved to the lower part of the narrow band—as usual in these circumstances—while the Italian lira moved to the upper part of the wide band and the French franc and the Irish pound moved to the upper part of the narrow band. The Belgian franc and the Danish krone remained in the lower part of the narrow band. In the wake of the realignment, interest rates fell in several countries as speculative trends were halted or reversed. The Central Bank of Ireland lowered the interest rate at which it provides short-term support to the money market by 1¼ percentage points immediately after the realignment, thus partly reversing an earlier increase. In Belgium, official rates were reduced in several steps in April and May. In Italy, the authorities lifted the foreign exchange restrictions introduced earlier to defend the lira and took additional measures to liberalize international capital movements. For several months following the realignment, the French franc remained strong with its divergence indicator above its upper threshold, while the deutsche mark and the Netherlands guilder alternated at the bottom of the narrow band. This opened in May the possibility for lower interest rates in France, but also required at times sizable obligatory exchange market interventions at the margin in support of the deutsche mark.[35] The Belgian franc and the Danish krone remained in the lower part of the narrow band in the three months after the realignment; the Irish pound, which had moved to the upper part of the narrow band, weakened subsequently, while the Italian lira remained almost unchanged in the upper part of the wide band. At the end of June, the deutsche mark and the Netherlands guilder began to strengthen and moved to the upper part of the narrow band in July. The Danish krone remained weak, and the Belgian franc moved somewhat higher.

On August 2, 1986, the Irish authorities requested a devaluation of the Irish pound by 8 percent vis-à-vis the other participating currencies, and the devaluation became effective on August 4. The Irish authorities had viewed with concern the decline in external competitiveness stemming from the sizeable appreciation of the Irish pound against the currencies of the United Kingdom and the United States since the April realignment, since these nations account for about 50 percent of Ireland's total external trade. Significant capital outflows occurred beginning in late June, and gross official reserves declined. Conditions in financial markets were somewhat unsettled in the period immediately preceding the realignment and money market interest rates, which had fallen considerably between April and June, tended to firm. In the first nine days following the realignment, the Irish pound moved to the top of the narrow band, and its exchange rate fell by 4½ percent against sterling and around 5 percent against the U.S. dollar.

An assessment of international competitiveness and its development in ERM countries since the inception of the system is fraught with many methodological difficulties. An often-used method is to look at the development of real effective exchange rates in terms of relative unit labor costs, GNP deflators, or consumer prices. This method can, of course, be criticized for not taking into account other than price-related determinants of international competitiveness (e.g., technology and marketing). Despite these limitations, it is noteworthy that exchange rate adjustments during the first eight years of operation of the EMS approximately offset or more than offset the changes in unit labor costs in the manufacturing sector and in consumer prices relative to ERM partner countries in Belgium, Denmark, France, the Federal Republic of Germany, and the Netherlands (Tables 11 and 13). The realignments did not, however, compensate the large accumulated unit labor cost and consumer price inflation differentials in Ireland and Italy. Relative to a broader sample of 16 industrial countries, however, the picture is less clear (Tables 12 and 14). While none of the ERM countries seems to have experienced a dramatic loss in international competitiveness as measured by relative unit labor costs adjusted for exchange rate changes, adjustments in exchange rates were not large enough in Ireland and Italy to compensate the increases in consumer prices vis-à-vis partner countries (Table 14).

---

[35] Only a small part of the debt stemming from these interventions was settled by the Bundesbank in official ECUs; the majority of the debt was settled later by the Bundesbank in U.S. dollars.

IV Variability of Exchange Rates

An assessment of exchange rate variability must be judgmental and is necessarily fraught with a variety of technical and conceptual difficulties. In this section, overall performance in terms of exchange rate variability is reviewed; the technical aspects are dealt with in a technical note at the end of this section. In order to assess the performance of the currencies participating in the EMS exchange rate mechanism, it would be desirable in principle to compare actual performance with estimated performance given the same exogenous world events, but in the absence of the EMS institutional apparatus. The requirements for constructing such a "counterfactual" experiment are, however, daunting. Therefore assessment has to be somewhat more limited and based on several elements: first, a comparison of exchange rate variability among the ERM currencies before and after the system's inception; second, a comparison of exchange rate variability between participating and nonparticipating currencies;[36] and third, an assessment of changes in exchange rate variability over time among the nonparticipating currencies. To the extent that a variety of different approaches all point in the same direction, some confidence can be placed in the results.

The broad conclusion of a previous analysis of exchange rate variability[37] was that ". . . it appears that the exchange rate variability of the EMS currencies has diminished since the introduction of the system . . . . In contrast, the exchange rate variability of the major currencies not tied to the EMS (the pound sterling, the U.S. dollar, and the Japanese yen) appears to have risen significantly." The present analysis differs from the former in four ways. First, the data used to perform the calculations have been extended by some three years. Second, the number of measures used to calculate variability has been increased (from one to three). Third, the changes in variability have been tested for statistical significance.[38] Fourth, several frequencies of exchange rate data (daily, weekly, and monthly) were examined to test the effect of data frequency on the measures of variability. This extended approach has broadly confirmed and strengthened the previous conclusions.

Conceptual Considerations

Interest in exchange rate variability arises from the belief that such variability imposes costs on economic agents. The nature of these costs is difficult to specify precisely, thus making agreement on an appropriate definition of variability also problematic. One argument is that exchange rate variations impose costs when they constitute variations away from equilibrium, in which case the variation around an equilibrium is the appropriate measure. There are, of course, great difficulties in attempting to define and measure equilibrium. It has been suggested that short-term swings of exchange rates around equilibrium are of minor importance, as the risks involved can be hedged, whereas medium- and long-term movements away from equilibrium may impose costly shifts in capital and labor resources between tradable and nontradable goods sectors, only for these shifts to be reversed as the exchange rate ultimately moves back. Indeed, such recent concern about exchange rate variability has, implicitly or explicitly, reflected a concern with the costs imposed by persistent and substantial deviations (overshooting or misalignments) of exchange rates from long-run equilibrium positions. Another argument is that unexpected exchange rate changes impose the most severe costs, in which case the relevant concept would be variation around an expected path, which also poses difficulties of measurement and interpretation. Measurement of the equilibrium exchange rate is beyond

---

[36] "Nonparticipating currencies" were selected on the basis of the importance of a currency in the international financial and trade system and the exchange rate regime of a country. The resulting group of eight currencies may, however, not be fully representative for all currencies outside the ERM of the EMS; this should be taken into account in the following comparison of exchange rate variability between the two groups. "Nonparticipating currencies" also refers to EC currencies not participating in the ERM, in particular the pound sterling (see also Section II).

[37] Ungerer (1983), p. 8–9.

[38] An alternative approach would be an analysis of variance. The F-test used here is intended to supplement the descriptive statistics on exchange rate variability provided in the Appendix Tables.

the scope of this study.[39] Instead, three different measures of exchange rate variability are employed, each with its own merits and drawbacks. The three measures are: the weighted average of the coefficient of variation[40] of bilateral exchange rates, the weighted average of the standard deviation of changes in the natural logarithm of bilateral exchange rates, and the standard deviation of changes in the natural logarithm of an effective exchange rate.[41] The properties of these measures are discussed further in the technical note at the end of this section.

The three measures are all calculated using nominal and real exchange rates (CPI based[42]), and variability of exchange rates is compared against ERM and non-ERM currencies. If bilateral rates move to offset relative inflation differentials, then variability of real exchange rates may capture more accurately the true risk to individuals than would variability of nominal rates. On the other hand, a major objective of the ERM has been to stabilize bilateral nominal exchange rates among participating currencies with the hope that the discipline of such a mechanism would lead to converging inflation rates and thus more stable real exchange rates as well. From this vantage point, the variability of actual nominal exchange rates is the more relevant approach in assessing the immediate success of the EMS. In a sense, the behavior of the real exchange rate over time provides a composite indicator of the behavior both of nominal exchange rates and relative inflation. Increased stability of real exchange rates could thus be an indication that nominal rate stability had been achieved and that there had been some convergence of inflation performance or that nominal exchange rate variations had closely matched divergence in inflation performance.

Patterns of Variability

The empirical results are presented in Tables 15–30, with Table 15 providing an overall summary. Tables 16–27 represent three versions of each of the three measures. Tables 28 and 29 are based on the Fund's multilateral exchange rate model's (MERM) effective

exchange rates. For these tables, monthly data were used while Table 30 employs daily data. Overall the picture that emerges is one of a decline, since 1979, in variability among the ERM currencies, an increase in variability among the non-ERM currencies, and also an increase in variability between the ERM and non-ERM currencies. Of course, within this overall picture there are diverging patterns.

Nominal Exchange Rate Variability

In Tables 16–18, where nominal exchange rate variability against ERM currencies is calculated, intra-ERM variability (for all ERM currencies) declined between the pre-EMS and EMS periods.[43] The drop in variability is particularly pronounced in the years 1983–85, as would be expected because of the more than two years that passed without a realignment. The changes in variability were statistically significant[44] for all ERM currencies except the Belgian/Luxembourg franc. This is a strong result.

For those countries not participating in the ERM, the variability of nominal exchange rates generally went up between the pre-EMS and EMS periods. In Table 18, six of eight non-ERM currencies showed an increase in variability, which was statistically significant for Sweden, the United Kingdom, and the United States—the latter showing the most pronounced rise of all. The Austrian schilling and Swiss franc were the two European non-ERM currencies to exhibit significant declines in nominal exchange rate variability against ERM currencies. For Austria, this probably reflects the authorities' aim of maintaining a close link between the schilling and the deutsche mark. Although the Swiss authorities have not targeted the exchange rate, the Swiss franc has in practice closely followed the deutsche mark. The pound sterling, which is a freely floating currency not linked to any of the ERM currencies, showed significant increases in nominal exchange rate variability against the ERM currencies.

In terms of nominal variability versus non-ERM currencies, almost all ERM currencies showed an increase in the ERM period, regardless of the measure chosen (Tables 22–24). Five of seven changes in nominal variability were statistically significant (excluding only the Federal Republic of Germany and Italy). When non-ERM currencies were compared with other non-ERM currencies, the pattern was less definitive. The U.S., U.K., and Japanese currencies all showed increases in nominal variability, which were

---

[39] See, however, D. Gros, "On the Volatility of Exchange Rates," Unpublished manuscript, International Monetary Fund, October 1986, for an attempt to determine overshooting of exchange rates.

[40] Standard deviation divided by the mean.

[41] In the second measure, the weighting is over the standard deviations, whereas in the third, the overall standard deviation is taken of an (already weighted) effective exchange rate. These measures of exchange rate variability do not, however, indicate whether the variability is the result of a large number of smaller changes or of only a few larger changes.

[42] For Ireland, wholesale price data were used for lack of monthly consumer price data.

[43] The period average is calculated as the average of yearly measures of variability.

[44] The 5 percent confidence level is used, unless otherwise stated.

statistically significant in the first two cases. Tables 28 and 29 show the variability of effective exchange rates against a wider group of currencies (those included in the MERM, that is, the 15 countries already included in the earlier tables plus Australia, Finland, and Spain). When the exchange rate variability of non-ERM currencies was measured against this larger group, the number of currencies indicating an increase in variability fell somewhat; two exhibited a significant increase—the United States and the United Kingdom. Of the ERM currencies, only France and Denmark exhibited an increase in variability of nominal effective exchange rates. None of the ERM currencies experienced a significant increase in variability.

As mentioned earlier, data frequency was also considered a factor that might influence measured patterns of variability. Table 30 provides the same set of computations as Table 16, but relies on daily instead of monthly exchange rate data; comparison makes it clear that data frequency has very little effect on measures of variability. Weekly data were also checked; the results (not reported here) were essentially the same as when daily data were used.

Real Exchange Rate Variability

Real exchange rate variability against ERM currencies is displayed in Tables 19–21. For the ERM currencies, real exchange rate variability against their own group fell for all currencies by all three measures, which is a strikingly uniform result. Only that for the Belgian/Luxembourg franc was not statistically significant, as had been the case for nominal exchange rate variability as well. A particularly noteworthy feature is the more clearly pronounced decline in intra-ERM real variability, compared with Ungerer (1983), which reflects the addition of the 1983–85 period, when there was greater convergence of inflation rates (see Section V).

For those countries not participating in the ERM, the variability of real exchange rates against ERM currencies went up between the pre-EMS and EMS periods. The same six countries that exhibited a rise in nominal exchange rate variability also saw real variability increase, especially that of the U.S. dollar. As with nominal variability, the Austrian schilling and the Swiss franc were the two European non-ERM currencies to exhibit significant declines in real exchange rate variability.

ERM currencies all showed an increase in variability of real exchange rates against non-ERM currencies between the pre- and post-1979 periods, irrespective of the measure used (Tables 25–27). The changes were,

however, statistically significant only for Belgium, France, and the Netherlands. Virtually all non-ERM currencies (excepting only Canada) showed an increase in real variability against their own group, with changes for Austria, Japan, United Kingdom, and United States statistically significant.

Conclusions

The aim of this analysis was to examine whether or not the establishment of the EMS coincided with a reduction in variability of exchange rates amongst ERM currencies. This question was assessed by an examination of several measures of variability before and after the establishment of the system for currencies inside and outside the exchange rate mechanism, and for both nominal and real exchange rates.

The strongest conclusion to be drawn from the study is that variability of bilateral exchange rates among ERM currencies has fallen since 1979, regardless of the measure chosen and irrespective of whether nominal or real rates were used in the calculations. In six of seven cases, the decline in measured variability was significant at the 1 percent confidence level (Tables 18 and 21).[45] This means that not only has the EMS succeeded in generating greater stability of nominal exchange rates, but also that to an increasing extent cost and price developments have converged (see also Section V).

Predictably the pattern was less striking with respect to the non-ERM currencies, both against ERM and against other non-ERM currencies. While intra-ERM variability appears to have decreased, the same cannot be said for intra-non-ERM variability. This result is not all that surprising because of the relative lack of homogeneity among the non-ERM countries as against the ERM countries. In Table 27, half the non-ERM currencies showed a statistically significant increase in variability against other non-ERM currencies.

The existence of the EMS since 1979 has coincided with a marked reduction in the variability of nominal and real exchange rates within the ERM. This was one major goal of the system, and for this purpose the intervention arrangements and other elements of the exchange rate mechanism were established. This trend toward greater stability, already evident in the earlier study undertaken in late 1982, has been substantially reinforced in the last three years, as there has been relative calm in the EMS exchange markets, as well

---

[45] This conclusion is all the more striking since some of the ERM currencies were participating in the European Common Margins Arrangement before 1979, which should also have had a constraining effect on variability in the earlier period.

as significant progress toward the goal of convergence of inflation rates.

By contrast, the variability of nominal and real exchange rates of participating versus nonparticipating currencies, and vice versa, has by and large stayed constant or risen. The nominal and real exchange rate variability of nonparticipating currencies against one another has shown no pronounced overall trend since 1979. Thus it does not seem that events exogenous to the EMS have led to the decline in exchange rate variability among participating currencies, since no such trend is evident elsewhere.[46] The clear diminution of exchange rate variability within the system, together with the absence of such a trend elsewhere, is certainly consistent with the view that the system has been successful in contributing to exchange rate stability among participating countries.

Technical Note: Measuring Exchange Rate Variability

This note presents the details of the measures of variability employed, as well as other aspects of the empirical work. One approach used is to examine stability around the average, that is, with no trend, which may be appropriate since a major aim of the system is to stabilize bilateral nominal rates. Another approach used is to assume that economic agents expect an underlying trend to continue in the near future. This allows the use of the variability of changes in the natural logarithm of the spot rate to be a proxy for "unexpected" changes.

Three measures of variability are employed: The weighted average of the coefficient of variation[47] of bilateral exchange rates, the weighted average of the standard deviation of changes in the natural logarithm of bilateral exchange rates, and the standard deviation of changes in the natural logarithm of an effective exchange rate. These three measures will be discussed in more detail below.

Any measure or definition of variability involves implicit assumptions that may be reasonable in some circumstances and not so reasonable in others. The choice is necessarily a matter of judgment and will, of course, depend on the notion of uncertainty that one has in mind. The three measures all have advantages and disadvantages, so that no single construct was relied upon. To the extent that several different measures indicate similar broad conclusions, it should be

reasonable to judge that the conclusions have at least some robustness and validity. A serious attempt was also made to assess the statistical significance of changes in exchange rate variability.[48]

Weighted Average of the Coefficients of Variation (CV) of the Bilateral Exchange Rates

If the bilateral exchange rate varies around a constant level, the coefficient of variation may be an appropriate measure of predictability, as it represents a measure of dispersion around the mean. In the ERM of the EMS, one of the goals is to keep relative nominal bilateral rates broadly constant, so that in this context also the CV may be appropriate as it measures the degree of success in achieving this goal.

Weighted Average of the Standard Deviation of Changes in the Natural Logarithm of the Exchange Rate (SD1)

If the exchange rate contains a trend, the SD1 measure may be more appropriate. This could happen when, for example, a currency continuously depreciates to offset an inflation differential. If market participants expect the exchange rate to follow a trend, variability around the expected trend captures best the risk to these traders. Clearly, variability around the mean, in this case, would be an inappropriate measure of risk.[49]

Standard Deviation of Changes in the Natural Logarithm of a Weighted Average of Bilateral Rates (SD2)

The SD2 measure differs from the SD1 measure in that it takes account of the covariance of bilateral

---

[46] This conclusion depends, however, on the assumption that the introduction of the EMS has not significantly affected exchange rate variations among nonparticipating countries.

[47] Standard deviation divided by the mean.

[48] Several earlier studies had shown exchange rate distributions to be leptokurtic—that is, more massive tails and a sharper peak than the normal distribution, which tends to invalidate many statistical procedures. However, K. Rogoff ("Can Exchange Rate Predictability be Achieved Without Monetary Convergence? Evidence from the EMS," *European Economic Review* (Amsterdam), Vol. 28 (1985), pp. 93–115) has indicated that "when mean absolute deviations rather than variances are used as a measure of variability, the comparisons across subperiods are qualitatively unaffected." Rogoff uses an F-statistic to test differences in conditional variances between subperiods. The same approach is employed here.

[49] It is possible, however, for an exchange rate to follow a medium-term trend away from the equilibrium or expected path, in which case the SD1 measure would be inappropriate. It is also possible for the determinants of the equilibrium to change quickly—for example, if there is an oil price shock—a case not allowed for by use of a smooth trend.

rates.[50] Inclusion of the covariance of bilateral rates can increase or decrease the measure of variability. For example, if two variables are positively (negatively) correlated, the variance of the sum of those two variables will be greater (less) than the sum of the variances of the two individual variables. Lanyi and Suss (1982) noted that in trying to capture changes in competitiveness a trade weighted VEER (variability of effective exchange rate) index is probably better than an EV (effective variability) index, since it takes into account the correlations in competitiveness among trading partners.[51] Since emphasis is placed on predictability and the cost of unexpected changes, if economic agents are aware of the covariances of bilateral exchange rates (as portfolio theory would suggest), this information should be taken into account in defining a measure of variability.

---

[50] The covariance is a measure of the extent to which two time series move together. The role of the covariance in the SD2 measure can be illustrated as follows:

$$VAR(\Sigma_j W_{ij} LN(S_{ij})) = \Sigma_j W_{ij}^2 VAR[LN(S_{ij})] \\ + 2\Sigma_j \Sigma_k W_{ij} W_{ik} COV[LN(S_{ij}),(S_{ik})]$$

where VAR = variance, COV = covariance, LN = natural logarithm, W_{ij} is the weight of currency j in the index of currency i, and S_{ij} is the bilateral rate between countries i and j.

[51] See A. Lanyi and E. Suss, "Exchange Rate Variability: Alternative Measures and Interpretation," *Staff Papers*, International Monetary Fund (Washington), Vol. 29 (December 1982), pp. 527–60.

V Economic Convergence Among EMS Member Countries

Conceptual Problems

In general terms, economic convergence can be defined as the narrowing of international differences in the development of economic variables. In the European context, the concept of economic convergence has been used in different ways with not always the same implications for the performance of economic variables. In referring to the ultimate objective of a fully economically integrated Europe, economic convergence has often been considered tantamount to convergence in living standards in EC member countries.[52] Although major differences in economic variables among European regions are expected to have diminished in an integrated Europe, differences in economic developments may be essential, even necessary, on the way to the final goal. It is, for example, unavoidable that relatively weaker regions maintain higher rates of real growth during the process of integration if they are to catch up with the relatively stronger regions.

On the other hand, economic convergence has been demanded in order to establish a sound basis for stable exchange rates among EC member countries, since these rates are often considered a prerequisite for further economic integration. Real growth differentials may, however, cause current account differentials that could require changes in exchange rates. Hence, it appears that requirements to achieve the intermediate objective of stable exchange rates may not always be consistent with those for reaching the final goal of full European economic integration. In practice, priority has been given to the achievement of the intermediate objective. Thus, economic convergence would in the first place imply a narrowing of international differences in the development of those economic variables that have a direct impact on exchange rate stability. This is the EMS concept of economic convergence.

There are two dimensions to this understanding of economic convergence: the narrowing of international differences in actual developments and the convergence of economic policy objectives. In general, the latter is a prerequisite for the former. Convergence of certain economic variables, such as inflation rates and growth of money supply, may sometimes appear more important than that of others, such as fiscal balances, for achieving stability in exchange rates. Moreover, the effects on exchange rates of divergences in some variables, for example, inflation rates, current account, and fiscal balances, can—at least in the short run—be neutralized by divergences in others, for example, interest rates and capital account balances. A scenario could be constructed in which divergences in these variables offset each other so that exchange rate stability would not be affected. Such situations could, however, be considered stable and sustainable in the longer run only if divergences in fiscal and current account balances are supported by consistent differences in the underlying saving-investment balances.[53] From this point of view, convergence of not only monetary variables but also to a certain degree of fiscal and current account balances appears to provide the best basis for stable exchange rates and consequent steps toward the final goal of economic integration. Other economic variables, such as real GDP growth and investment, however, can only be expected to converge if divergences are attributable to differences in monetary and fiscal policies and do not reflect differences in underlying economic fundamentals (e.g., factor endowments and rate of technical progress).

There is a debate about the line of reference on which economic variables should converge. Although no universally accepted formula exists, there appears to be a consensus for "monetary stability at home" implying that economic variables, in particular inflation rates, should not simply converge toward the EC average, but rather move in a direction consistent with a high degree of price stability.[54] In practice, this implies that the country with the lowest rate of inflation sets the standards for others.[55]

---

[52] See Preamble to EEC Treaty; see also Ungerer (1983), p. 10.

[53] See V. Tanzi and T. Ter-Minassian, "The European Monetary System and Fiscal Policies," Paper presented to the conference on tax coordination in the EEC held in Rotterdam, August 22–24, 1985 (forthcoming).

[54] See Ungerer (1983), p. 10.

[55] See Russo, *ibid.*

From the above considerations it follows that an empirical investigation of economic convergence among countries participating in the exchange rate mechanism of the EMS over the recent years should address two questions:

1. Has convergence of monetary and real variables as well as policy variables that have a bearing on exchange rate stability improved among these countries?
2. Have there been any slippages in the attempt to contain inflation as a result of the pursuit of exchange rate stability?

Answers to these questions would allow an assessment as to whether the EMS has provided a sound basis for exchange rate stability among its member countries.

Economic analysis of these questions should ideally attempt to establish some counterfactual evidence to the actual developments, that is, provide estimates of economic developments in EMS countries under the assumed absence of the exchange rate mechanism. By comparing actual with counterfactual variables, the contribution of the EMS to economic convergence and price stability could be assessed. Detailed modelling of EMS economies, which would allow simulation of counterfactual developments is, however, difficult, and perhaps even impossible with available analytical tools.

Widely used and simple techniques to study the effects of economic policies are to compare developments in economic variables before and after the implementation of measures or to compare developments between economies affected and those not affected ("control group") by these measures. Obviously, a major shortcoming of the first technique is the assumption that in the period of investigation no other factors influenced economic developments than the change in economic policy. The second technique rests on the equally unrealistic assumption that differences in the developments of economies affected by the policy and the control group result only from the policy measures taken in the group under study. While results obtained with either of these techniques may not appear very convincing, some confidence can perhaps be placed in results that are supported by both approaches. Effects of an economic policy would then be assessed on the basis of observed differences in economic developments during the time periods before and after the measures were implemented, and between the group of countries affected by these measures and a control group.

This technique is applied to determine whether the introduction of the EMS has been followed by improved economic convergence among countries participating in the exchange rate mechanism of the EMS. The period 1974–84/85 is split into a pre-EMS period

(1974–78) and an EMS period (1979–84/85).[56] The control group comprises—dependent on data availability—15 industrial countries, including the United Kingdom, Greece, Spain, and Portugal, which, although they are members of the EC, do not participate in the ERM. The monetary variables considered are changes in consumer prices, GDP deflators, unit labor costs, domestic credit, narrow and broad money (both in nominal and real terms), and interest rates. Moreover, central government budget balances and external current account balances are compared. Real sector variables considered are real GDP growth and gross fixed capital formation. Among these variables, nominal domestic credit and money, fiscal balances, and interest rates are sometimes regarded by national authorities as policy instruments or intermediate policy targets.

The following reviews price, monetary, fiscal, external current account, and real sector developments in ERM and other industrial countries. Ungerer (1983) investigated economic convergence in EMS countries during 1974–81 and came to the following conclusion:

> It had been hoped that the EMS would promote greater convergence of economic policies and developments and eventually facilitate economic integration. So far, however, such hopes have not been fulfilled as convergence of policies, particularly budgetary and monetary policies, has been insufficient to maintain a high degree of exchange rate stability. The lack of coordination of policies has been reflected in a lack of convergence of economic performance and, in particular, of cost and price developments. An opinion held by many, however, is that the existence of and the constraints imposed by the EMS have helped to prevent a greater divergence of economic developments in the participating countries.[57]

Price Developments

Price developments, measured as annual percentage changes of consumer price indices and GDP deflators, follow the same pattern in ERM and non-ERM countries during the period 1974–85, (Tables 31 and 32).

---

[56] This implies a certain simplification of historical developments which cannot easily be pressed into two distinct time periods. Convergence in economic developments may have already existed between some participants in the European Common Margins Arrangement before 1979. Also, economic convergence may have improved more recently as compared with the early years of the EMS.

[57] Further empirical evidence on these issues can be found in A. Steinherr, "Convergence and Coordination of Macroeconomic Policies: Some Basic Issues," *European Economy* (Brussels), No. 20 (July 1984), pp. 71–110, M. Wegner, "Das EWS - ein Teilerfolg," *IFO-Schnelldienst*, 17–18/85, pp. 15–25, and the studies quoted in Ungerer (1983).

There was a general surge in inflation rates after the first round of oil price increases, which then subsided during 1976–79. The second jump in oil prices in 1979 accelerated inflation for about a year before it receded again.

After the first round of oil price increases of 1973/74 had worked its way through the economies of future ERM member countries, inflation differentials narrowed at least in absolute terms (see standard deviations and differences between highest and lowest price changes within ERM countries in Tables 31 and 32). But the launching of the EMS in 1979 roughly coincided with the second increase of oil prices, which caused an intensification of inflationary pressure. The response to this pressure varied considerably between ERM countries, leading to a renewed increase in inflation differentials in the following year. The difference between the highest and the lowest rate of inflation peaked in 1980 when consumer prices rose by only 5 percent in the Federal Republic of Germany as against 21 percent in Italy. From around 1981 onwards, however, inflation differentials narrowed in absolute terms (Chart 5). In 1985, Germany's inflation rate was only 2 percent, down from 6 percent in 1981, while that of Ireland and Italy decreased to around 5 and 9 percent, down from more than 18 and 21 percent, respectively, in 1980. Hence, in 1985, inflation differentials between ERM countries reached their lowest value since 1974.

The development of inflation differentials in selected countries outside the ERM was somewhat different. Altogether, inflation differentials did not narrow, either in absolute or in relative terms, on average during the 1974–85 period, although there was improved convergence in more recent years. A regional breakdown shows that inflation differentials even widened in the groups of southern European countries (Greece, Portugal, and Spain) and countries in the Pacific area (Australia, Japan, and New Zealand). They narrowed, however, among countries of the Atlantic area (Canada, United Kingdom, and United States)[58] and among central European and Scandinavian countries (Austria, Finland, Norway, Sweden, and Switzerland).[59] It is noteworthy that inflation rates of central European and Scandinavian countries moved closer in line with those of ERM countries than with inflation rates of Atlantic countries. This reflects the rather strong orientation of economic policies of central and northern European countries with those of ERM countries, while Canada and the United Kingdom seem to have followed policies more similar to policies of the United States. Taken together, it appears that the desire for

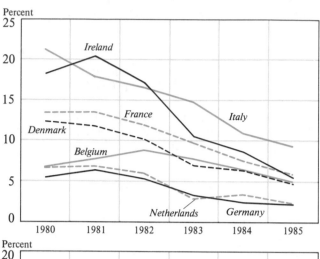

Chart 5. Rates of Inflation[1] in EMS and Selected Other Industrial Countries

Percent

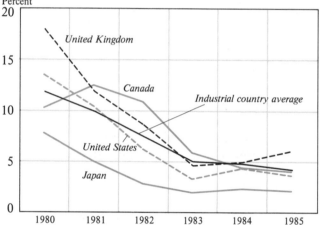

Source: International Monetary Fund, *International Financial Statistics*, various issues.

[1] Measured as percentage changes in consumer prices.

convergence in inflation rates was somewhat stronger in ERM countries (and in countries that followed economic policies similar to policies of ERM countries) than in countries outside the ERM,[60] but this tendency might, at least to some extent, already have existed before the EMS was formally launched.[61]

The average rate of inflation in ERM countries was lower than that of those non-ERM countries examined here throughout the 1974–85 period. Moreover, inflation fell somewhat more in ERM countries on average in the second sub-period, in particular in more recent

---

[58] See Chart 5.

[59] Because of a persistent high rate of inflation and special features of its economy, Iceland was not included in any of the four regional groupings of non-ERM countries.

[60] There was, however, a rather close convergence of inflation rates between the United States, United Kingdom, and Canada in 1979–84.

[61] An exchange rate arrangement similar to the EMS—the European Common Margins Arrangement—already existed between several European countries before 1979. This might have constrained domestic monetary policies in some countries and contributed to convergence of inflation rates in 1974–78.

years, than in non-ERM countries. While this observation by itself cannot be taken to imply that the EMS has fostered price stability in participating countries, it certainly weakens the arguments of those who predicted that anti-inflationary policies would become less effective in the framework of the EMS. A more formal, even though rather crude, test of the inflationary effects of the EMS was performed by estimating a simple annual inflation model in a pooled time-series cross-sectional analysis for the complete group of 22 industrial countries, including countries participating in the ERM, for the period 1974–84 and making use of a dummy variable that takes the value of 1 for every observation (country/year) under the ERM and 0 otherwise.[62] The dummy variable appeared in all estimated equations with a negative coefficient, which was statistically significant at the 5 percent or 1 percent level in most cases (Tables 33–35).[63] This exercise seems to support the hypothesis that the EMS has not laid the ground for looser monetary policies but rather provided a framework in which anti-inflationary policies could be pursued more effectively.[64]

The development in unit labor costs was similar in ERM and other countries (Table 36). In both groups, unit labor costs increased less on average in 1979–85 than in 1974–78, but the reduction was higher in the group of other countries than in ERM countries. Moreover, international differences in unit labor cost developments narrowed significantly in absolute terms in other countries but only slightly in ERM countries.

---

[62] The model used was of the following form:

$$p = a_0 + a_1 \, \mathrm{gdp} + a_2 m + a_3 \, pe + a_4 \, \mathrm{dummy}$$

where p = rate of inflation, gdp = growth of real GDP/GNP, m = growth of (narrow/broad) money, pe = expected rate of inflation, dummy = EMS dummy variable, and a_2, a_3 are assumed to be positive while a_1 is assumed to be negative. This model is based on a very simple demand for money function, which does not take into account portfolio decisions, and on the assumption of exogenous money supply and endogenous prices. While the latter assumption may seem appropriate for countries with flexible exchange rates, its validity can be questioned for EMS countries. Indeed, if the EMS would be regarded as a fixed exchange rate system, it could be argued that the above model would be misspecified for EMS countries. There are, however, at least two reasons why it was felt that the model was also appropriate for EMS countries. First, the EMS was not designed as, and has never become, a fixed exchange rate system in the classical sense; in fact, it was characterized by periodical realignments. Second, there are still substantial restrictions of international capital flows between major EMS member countries which allow a certain degree of independence—and divergence—in monetary policies.

[63] Regressions were run over (1) all observations, i.e., the pooled time series-cross section data for the 22 countries in 1974–84, (2) observations for all countries in 1979–84, and (3) observations for ERM countries in 1974–84. Overall, econometric estimates of the model of inflation seemed satisfactory given the crude nature of the exercise.

[64] Before firm conclusions can be drawn, this illustrative exercise should be complemented by more detailed country studies of the constraints from the EMS on domestic monetary policies. This would, however, go beyond the scope of this paper.

Monetary Developments

In ERM countries, monetary expansion slowed in the 1980s; growth rates for narrow and broad money fell by about 4 to 5 percentage points on average in 1979–84 as compared with 1974–78 (Tables 37 and 38). Monetary restraint was most pronounced in Belgium, the Federal Republic of Germany, and the Netherlands; it was less strict in France and Italy, where both narrow and broad money grew annually by more than 10 percent in 1979–84. In Denmark, monetary expansion even accelerated in recent years, reaching a peak in 1984 (Chart 6).

Other countries, taken together, experienced broadly unchanged narrow money and even higher broad money growth on average in 1979–84 as compared with 1974–78. The regional breakdown shows that narrow money growth was somewhat smaller on average in central European, Scandinavian, and Pacific-area countries than in Southern European and Atlantic-area countries. Broad money expanded on average at almost the same rate in the two time periods in the group of central European and Scandinavian countries. Growth of broad money was, however, higher in the more recent period in southern European and Atlantic-area countries, while it was lower on average in countries of the Pacific area.

Differences in narrow money expansion were somewhat higher in ERM countries in 1979–85 as compared with 1974–78 but almost doubled in the group of other countries. On a regional basis, international differences in narrow money growth increased on average in the groupings of central European and Scandinavian countries, southern European countries, and countries in the Pacific area, but they narrowed significantly between the United States, the United Kingdom, and Canada. Differences in broad money expansion between ERM countries declined in 1979–84, at least in absolute terms (as measured by average standard deviations). They widened significantly, however, between other countries. Within this group, only central European and Scandinavian countries experienced fewer differences in broad money developments between each other during the more recent period.

A better measure of convergence in monetary policies is perhaps the spread in nominal domestic credit expansion since this expansion largely excludes the frequently offsetting influence of the external sector. In ERM countries absolute differences declined on average in 1979–84 as compared with 1974–78 (Table 39). Moreover, Belgium, the Federal Republic of Germany, and the Netherlands achieved almost the same rate of domestic credit expansion in 1984. Although France slightly reduced domestic credit in that year, Denmark, Ireland, and Italy followed policies

Chart 6. Growth of Narrow Money in EMS and Other Industrial Countries

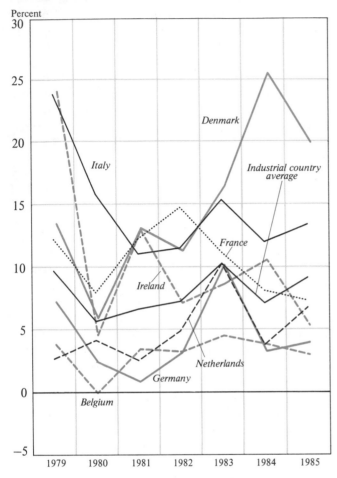

Source: International Monetary Fund, *International Financial Statistics*, various issues.

allowing domestic credit to expand by double digit rates.

The spread in nominal domestic credit expansion increased sharply in the group of other countries. As the regional breakdown shows, however, there were more similarities within regional groupings than across country groups. In almost all groups, with the exception of southern European countries, international differences in domestic credit expansion narrowed in absolute as well as in relative terms in 1979–84 as compared with 1974–78.

Monetary variables deflated by the consumer price index combine features of monetary policy variables with the induced actual price developments. While there was a sharp reduction of growth of real narrow and broad money as well as real domestic credit expansion in ERM countries during 1979–84 over the 1974–78 period, real money and credit growth changed

only slightly or accelerated in other countries (Tables 40–42). Differences in real narrow money growth diminished neither in ERM nor in other countries, but there appeared to be some narrowing of differences of real broad money and real domestic credit growth in other (though not in ERM) countries.

Both short-term and long-term interest rates rose and interest differentials widened in ERM and other countries in 1979–84 as compared with 1974–78 (Tables 43 and 44). While short-term interest rate differentials appeared to have narrowed in ERM countries in absolute as well as in relative terms in 1984, the opposite seems to have occurred in selected other countries (but the sample size is too small to give much weight to this finding).

Differences between ERM and non-ERM member countries are less pronounced with regard to long-term interest rates. Interest rate differentials increased moderately in both groups in relative as well as in absolute terms in 1979–84 as compared with 1974–78.

In most ERM countries, with the exception of France and Italy, short-term interest rates moved more closely with those of partner countries in 1979–84 than in 1974–78 (Table 45). The smaller countries, Belgium, Denmark, and the Netherlands, all followed policies that brought their short-term interest rates closer in line with German interest rates while for some of these countries the relationship with French and Italian rates loosened. Regarding long-term interest rates, correlation was in all cases substantially stronger in 1979–85 than in 1974–78 (Table 46). Although interest rate developments in the United States played a significant role,[65] a large part of the closer relationship of interest rates among ERM countries can be attributed to the way monetary policy has been conducted following the establishment of the EMS. The Federal Republic of Germany and other larger ERM countries have used the rate of growth of monetary aggregates as an intermediate objective of monetary policy. Smaller ERM countries with very open economies and the determination to contain inflation have often targeted the deutsche mark exchange rate with the result that their interest rate developments converged with German developments; monetary expansion in these countries, on the other hand, has remained largely outside the control of the national authorities. More recently, France has sought to follow similar policies.

---

[65] Indeed, with exceptionally high U.S. interest rates over the recent years, European countries had to choose a trade-off between the objectives of stimulating investment and growth by lower interest rates and of containing capital outflows and strengthening their currencies against the U.S. dollar in order to lower inflationary pressures.

Fiscal and External Current Account Developments

In contrast to some improvements in economic convergence among ERM countries in price and some monetary variables, differences in fiscal policies and developments do not seem to have been overcome. Average fiscal deficits widened in ERM countries in 1979–84 as compared with 1974–78 (Table 47). The major reasons for this development were increasing deficits in Italy and Belgium and continuing high deficits in Ireland. The increase in average deficits was accompanied by an increase in differences in fiscal balances. On average, standard deviations and differences between highest and lowest deficits were somewhat higher in 1979–84 than in 1974–78. This was mainly because Germany succeeded in reducing its central government budget deficit to 1.6 percent of GDP in 1984 while the Italian government boosted its deficit to almost 16 percent.

Deficits also increased in other countries, from around 3½ percent on average in 1974–78 to about 4 percent in 1979–84. The increase was much smaller than in the ERM group however and budget deficits remained well below the levels reached in some ERM countries. Moreover, the international spread of budget deficits rose only slightly in absolute terms and remained constant in relative terms in this country grouping.

The external current account performance worsened significantly in ERM countries in 1979–84 as compared with 1974–78. While average current account balances were in surplus in the earlier period, they were in deficit by about US$2 billion in the more recent period (Table 48). Only the Netherlands succeeded in improving its average current account balance in 1979–84 over 1974–78, in large part because of its special situation as an energy exporter. Other countries, notably Germany, on average experienced a severe weakening in their current account performance.[66] The deterioration in the external accounts of EMS countries was accompanied by more uniformity; the spread between average current account positions was significantly smaller in 1979–84 as compared with 1974–78.

Countries outside the ERM, too, experienced a weakening in their average current account performance. While the deterioration was much smaller than for the group of EMS countries, however, international divergences in this group increased significantly both in absolute and relative terms (Table 48).

Real Sector Developments

Both gross fixed capital formation as a percentage of GDP and real growth were lower in ERM countries on average in 1979–84 than in 1974–78 (Tables 49 and 50). While divergences in real growth rates narrowed somewhat in absolute terms, differences in investment performance widened both in absolute and relative terms.

Developments in the control group of countries not participating in the exchange rate mechanism of the ERM were somewhat different. On average, growth rates did not change much in the two subperiods of 1974–84, but, as happened in the group of EMS countries, gross fixed capital formation as a percentage of GDP was somewhat lower in the more recent period. Also, it appears that both growth and investment differentials narrowed on average in 1979–84 as compared with 1974–78.

Conclusions

The above statistics and calculations have illustrated that there has been progress within the EMS toward economic convergence in domestic monetary policies and inflation rates, particularly in the more recent years. Improvement in these areas was recorded against a "control group" of countries not participating in the ERM or against conditions in the pre-EMS period 1974–78. Moreover, better convergence among ERM countries has not been accompanied by more inflationary policies. Rather, there has been a general trend toward more restrictive financial policies.

The recent improvement in convergence in inflation rates and monetary policies, however, has not been backed by corresponding progress in the fiscal sector and the external current account nor with regard to real sector developments. In particular, fiscal deficits in ERM countries widened on average in the early 1980s, and differences between ERM countries increased. The apparent lack of progress toward economic convergence in these areas introduces an element of uncertainty into the EMS and in the medium run may jeopardize its main objective of providing members with reliable and stable exchange rate relationships.

---

[66] The Federal Republic of Germany, after having agreed at the 1979 economic summit meeting to stimulate its economy, had a record current account deficit in 1980 (1.9 percent of GNP) which caused a weakening of the deutsche mark in the EMS. The authorities resisted a devaluation of the deutsche mark and tightened monetary policy instead (see Table 39). By 1982, they had succeeded in turning the current account into a sizeable and growing surplus, which reached 38.8 billion deutsche mark in 1985 (equivalent to 2.1 percent of GNP).

Appendix I
Statistical Tables

Table 1.   Quotas and Ceilings Under the Short-Term Monetary Support and Medium-Term Financial Assistance Facilities

Countries	Debtor and Creditor Quotas Under Short-Term Monetary Support			Commitment (Creditor) Ceilings Under Medium-Term Financial Assistance	
	Debtor *(In millions of ECUs)*	Creditor	Percentage Distribution	Amount *(In millions of ECUs)*	Percentage Distribution
Belgium/Luxembourg	580	1,160	6.50	1,035	6.50
Denmark	260	520	2.91	465	2.92
France	1,740	3,480	19.51	3,105	19.50
Germany, Fed. Rep. of	1,740	3,480	19.51	3,105	19.50
Greece	150	300	1.68	270	1.69
Ireland	100	200	1.12	180	1.13
Italy	1,160	2,320	13.00	2,070	13.00
Netherlands	580	1,160	6.50	1,035	6.50
Portugal	145	290	1.63	259	1.63
Spain	725	1,450	8.13	1,294	8.13
United Kingdom	1,740	3,480	19.51	3,105	19.50
Total EC	**8,920**	**17,840**	**100.00**	**15,923**	**100.00**

Source: Committee of the Governors of the Central Banks of the Member States of the European Economic Community—European Monetary Cooperation Fund, *Texts Concerning the European Monetary System* (Brussels, 1985).

Table 2. The Creation of ECUs by Swap Operations, 1979–86

Swap Operations Starting In		Gold Transfers (*Million ounces*)	U.S. Dollar Transfers (*Billions*)	Gold Price (*ECUs per ounce*)	US$1 Per ECU	Counterpart in ECUs (*Billions*)		
						Gold	U.S. dollars	Total
1979	II	80.7	13.4	165	0.75	13.3	10.0	**23.3**
1979[1]	III	85.3	15.9	185	0.73	15.8	11.6	**27.4**
1979	IV	85.3	16.0	211	0.70	18.0	11.3	**29.3**
1980	I	85.5	15.5	259	0.69	22.2	10.7	**32.9**
1980	II	85.6	14.4	370	0.77	31.7	11.1	**42.8**
1980	III	85.6	13.7	419	0.70	35.9	9.6	**45.5**
1980	IV	85.6	13.9	425	0.71	36.4	9.9	**46.3**
1981	I	85.6	14.5	447	0.75	38.3	10.9	**49.2**
1981	II	85.7	14.2	440	0.84	37.7	12.0	**49.7**
1981	III	85.7	12.7	406	0.97	34.8	12.3	**47.1**
1981	IV	85.7	11.5	402	0.91	34.5	10.5	**45.0**
1982	I	85.7	11.7	368	0.92	31.6	10.7	**42.3**
1982	II	85.7	10.5	327	1.00	28.0	10.5	**38.6**
1982	III	85.7	9.9	324	1.04	27.8	10.3	**38.1**
1982	IV	85.7	10.0	367	1.08	31.5	10.8	**42.3**
1983	I	85.7	10.0	429	1.02	36.7	10.2	**47.0**
1983	II	85.7	10.5	452	1.07	38.8	11.2	**50.0**
1983	III	85.7	10.5	465	1.13	39.9	11.8	**51.7**
1983	IV	85.7	10.6	477	1.15	40.9	12.2	**53.1**
1984	I	85.7	10.6	461	1.24	39.5	13.1	**52.6**
1984	II	85.7	10.8	452	1.17	38.7	12.7	**51.4**
1984	III	85.7	10.6	460	1.26	39.5	13.3	**52.8**
1984	IV	85.7	10.1	454	1.35	39.0	13.6	**52.6**
1985	I	85.7	10.2	434	1.42	37.2	14.5	**51.7**
1985	II	85.7	9.0	449	1.40	38.5	12.6	**51.1**
1985	III	85.7	10.0	429	1.35	36.8	13.5	**50.3**
1985	IV	86.5	10.5	396	1.19	34.0	12.5	**46.5**
1986	I	86.5	10.6	368	1.13	31.8	12.0	**43.8**
1986	II	86.5	11.2	373	1.09	32.3	12.3	**44.6**

Source: Commission of the European Communities.
[1] The Bank of England transferred 20 percent of its gold and U.S. dollar reserves from July 1979.

Table 3. Percentage Weights of Member Currencies in the ECU[1]

(Annual second quarter average)

	1975[2]	1979	1980	1981	1982	1983	1984	1985	1986
Belgian franc	8.0	9.1	9.1	8.8	8.1	8.1	8.0	8.2	8.4
Danish krone	3.0	3.0	2.8	2.7	2.7	2.7	2.6	2.7	2.8
French franc	21.7	19.7	19.7	19.1	18.3	16.9	16.7	19.2	19.1
Deutsche mark	26.9	32.8	32.9	32.7	34.7	36.5	37.0	32.0	33.3
Irish pound	1.4	1.1	1.1	1.1	1.1	1.1	1.0	1.2	1.2
Italian lira	13.3	9.7	9.2	8.6	8.2	8.1	7.9	9.8	9.5
Luxembourg franc	0.3	0.3	0.3	0.3	0.3	0.3	0.3	0.3	0.3
Netherlands guilder	9.1	10.4	10.3	10.2	10.8	11.2	11.4	10.1	10.6
Pound sterling	16.1	13.8	14.5	16.5	15.7	15.1	14.8	15.1	13.7
Greek drachma	—	—	—	—	—	—	—	1.2	0.9
Total	100.0	100.0	100.0	100.0	100.0	100.0	100.0	100.0	100.0

Memorandum:

Value of 1 ECU in terms of:

Belgian franc	45.53	40.34	40.36	41.43	45.10	45.23	45.61	45.12	43.94
Danish krone	7.16	7.15	7.83	7.97	8.13	8.08	8.21	8.05	7.84
French franc	5.29	5.83	5.85	6.03	6.29	6.81	6.87	6.83	6.85
Deutsche mark	3.08	2.52	2.51	2.54	2.38	2.27	2.24	2.25	2.16
Irish pound	0.55	0.66	0.67	0.69	0.69	0.72	0.73	0.72	0.71
Italian lira	819.45	1,128.65	1,182.76	1,263.36	1,321.97	1,346.57	1,382.75	1,429.76	1,475.67
Luxembourg franc	45.53	40.34	40.36	41.43	45.10	45.23	45.61	45.12	43.94
Netherlands guilder	3.14	2.75	2.76	2.81	2.64	2.55	2.52	2.53	2.42
Pound sterling	0.55	0.64	0.61	0.54	0.56	0.59	0.59	0.58	0.64
Greek drachma	—	—	—	—	—	—	—	98.54	135.01
U.S. dollar	1.29	1.33	1.39	1.12	1.00	0.91	0.83	0.73	0.96
Japanese yen	292.40	290.06	322.39	245.41	244.66	216.65	189.48	182.17	163.24
Swiss franc	2.57	2.28	2.34	2.27	2.00	1.89	1.85	1.88	1.79

Sources: International Monetary Fund, *International Financial Statistics*, various issues; and Fund staff calculations.

[1] Calculations of percentage weights are based on New York noon quotations. The weights may not add up because of rounding.

[2] Weights are those of the European Unit of Account (EUA), which was introduced in certain areas of EC activities as of April 21, 1975. The EUA is defined as a basket of all EC currencies; this basket was also used for defining the ECU in 1979.

Table 4. Composition of the ECU

	National Currency Units		Percentage Weights[1]		
	March 13, 1979– September 14, 1984	September 17, 1984	March 13, 1979	September 14, 1984	September 17, 1984
Belgian franc	3.66	3.71	9.3	8.1	8.2
Danish krone	0.217	0.219	3.1	2.7	2.7
French franc	1.15	1.31	19.8	16.7	19.0
Deutsche mark	0.828	0.719	33.0	36.9	32.0
Irish pound	0.00759	0.00871	1.1	1.0	1.2
Italian lira	109.00	140.00	9.5	7.9	10.2
Luxembourg franc	0.14	0.14	0.4	0.3	0.3
Netherlands guilder	0.286	0.256	10.5	11.3	10.1
Pound sterling	0.0885	0.0878	13.3	15.1	15.0
Greek drachma	—	1.15	—	—	1.3
			100.0	100.0	100.0

Sources: Council Regulation (EEC) No. 3180/78 of December 18, 1978; Council Regulation (EEC) No. 2626/84 and Council Declaration of September 15, 1984; Fund staff calculations.

[1] Based on market rates.

Table 5.   EMS: Periods of Strain[1]

No.	Period	Source of Strain	Signaled by Divergence indicator[2]	Signaled by Parity grid	Remedies Adopted
1	May–June 1979	D: Widening CA deficits and deficient capital inflow. B: Continued lack of confidence.	DKr: −75	DM/BF	Intervention to support both BF and DKr. B: Discount rate up from 6 to 9 percent. D: Discount rate up from 8 to 9 percent.
2	Aug.–Sept. 1979	D and B: Capital inflows induced by earlier increases in nominal interest rates dry out in both countries.	DKr: −75 BF: −75	DM/DKr	Intervention to support both BF and DKr. D: Discount rate up from 9 to 11 percent on Sept. 17 after which date intervention stops. B: Discount rate up from 9 to 10 percent. Realignment I: DM up, DKr down relative to other EMS currencies.
3	Nov. 1979	Uncertainty after parliamentary election in late October puts pressure on the DKr.	DKr: slightly negative fews days before realignment.		Intervention in support of DKr. Realignment II: DKr devalued against all other EMS currencies.
4	Dec. 1979– March 1980	D: Deficient capital inflow because of uncertainty about DKr in view of two recent realignments and because of increasing international nominal interest rates. B: Deficient capital inflow to finance CA deficits.		FF/BF (in March)	Intervention keeps DKr in the middle of the band. Discount rate up from 11 to 13 percent. B: Intervention majority in EMS currencies to support BF. Discount rate up from 10 to 14 percent.
5	Oct. 1980	G: Weak CA position relative to U.S. and major EMS countries plus interest differential disfavoring DM denominated investments.	DM: −70	FF/DM	Intervention in support of DM. F: Loosening of credit market. G: Slight tightening of credit market.
6	Feb. 1981	G: As U.S. interest rates surge and uncertainty about G's strategic (Poland) and economical position increases, pressure on DM becomes heavy.	DM: −60s FF: touching +75 occasionally in Jan. and Feb.	FF/BF and FF/BF	Intervention in $ and FF to support DM. G: Special Lombard rate introduced; substantial tightening of monetary policy.
7	March 1981	BF and Lit exposed at bottom of band subsequent to DM firming. After devaluation of Lit, BF remains under heavy pressure.	BF: −75 Lit: −75 (briefly)	DM/BF and FF/BF	I: Intervention followed by increase in discount rate from 16.5 to 19 percent. Realignment III: Devaluation of Lit. B: Intervention followed by increase in the discount rate from 12 to 16 percent.
8	May 1981	Presidential election in France (5/10/81).	FF: −75 (two weeks from 5/11/81)	DM/FF	F: Intervention. Interest rate and exchange control measures.
9	Aug.–Sept. 1981	On the background of pessimism as to the devaluation of the FF, DM gains strength on improving external performance, and FF and BF have problems following DM up against $.	DM: +75 (last two weeks of Sept.) BF: not past −75 but most "diverging" of weak currencies.	DM/BF	Intervention in support of weak EMS currencies. Realignment IV: DM and f. revalued and FF and Lit devalued against DKr, BF, £Ir.
10	Nov. 1981	Brief pressure on BF when negotiations to form a government break down.	BF: once below −75 on Dec. 10.		Intervention in support of BF. B: Discount rate from 13 to 15 percent.
11	Feb. 1982	Diminishing confidence in the future performance of the Belgian economy.	BF: close to, but not past −75 DKr: slightly negative		B: Intervention. Realignment V: Devaluation of BF and DKr against other EMS currencies.

Table 5 (*Concluded*).   **EMS: Periods of Strain[1]**

No.	Period	Source of Strain	Signaled by		Remedies Adopted
			Divergence indicator[2]	Parity grid	
12	March 1982	F: Widening inflation differential with G. DKr and BF lose strength acquired in previous realignments.	FF: one flash (-76) on March 23; otherwise well within bounds.	DM/FF and f./FF	F: Intervention, tightening of monetary policy, exchange controls, budget tightening.
13	May–June 1982	"The weekend syndrome": pressure on BF, FF, Lit, especially late in week. Persistent realignment rumors.	DM: above $+75$ from end-April. BF: most "diverging" currency at bottom.	DM/BF	Intervention. Realignment VI: Revaluation of DM and f. and devaluation of Lit and FF against DKr, BF, and £Ir.
14	Dec. 1982–March 1983	Deteriorating trade balance and inflation in France. Increasing pressure on FF, especially late in week; persistent realignment rumors; anticipation of realignment after March elections in Federal Republic of Germany, France.	BF: frequently below in January, February; FF: below in March.	DM/FF f./BF	Substantial intervention in support of BF and FF, interest rate measures in Belgium, Federal Republic of Germany, Netherlands. Emergency foreign exchange measures in Belgium. Realignment VII: Revaluation of DM, f., DKr, BF, and devaluation of FF, Lit, £Ir.
15	March–July 1985	Significant deterioration in performance of the Italian economy in the fiscal and external accounts puts Lit under pressure.	Lit: -40 Movement of the lira to the lower part of the wide band.	DKr/Lit	Realignment VIII: Devaluation of Lit by about 8 percent against other participating currencies.
16	Dec. 1985–Jan. 1986	Weak performance of the Italian and Belgian economies and realignment rumors; decline of sterling against participating currencies.	£Ir: From 0 to -60 BF: -75 Drop of £Ir to bottom of narrow band; further downward pressure on BF; decline of Lit from its strong position after Realignment VIII.	DM/BF	Substantial intervention in support of BF; increase in Belgian and Irish interest rates; tightening on monetary policy and foreign exchange restrictions in Italy.
17	April 4, 1986	F: Widening inflation differential particularly with Germany; realignment initiated by new government.	FF and £Ir fall below their lower intervention limits, DM and f. rise above their upper intervention limits.	. . .	Realignment IX: Revaluation of DM. f., BF, and DKr; devaluation of FF.
18	August 2, 1986	Ire: Depreciation of $ and sterling against ERM currencies endangers competitive position of the Irish economy.	£Ir: from 16 to -37	FF/DKr	Realignment X: Devaluation of £Ir by about 8 percent against other participating currencies.

Source: Fund staff estimates and calculations.

[1] Defined as periods with reports of substantial interference in the exchange market by intervention, capital and exchange controls, or measures of monetary policy motivated by exchange rate developments. Notation: B—Belgium; BF—Belgian franc; D—Denmark; DKr—Danish krone; F—France; FF—French franc; G—Federal Republic of Germany; DM—deutsche mark; Ire—Ireland; £Ir—Irish pound; I—Italy; Lit—Italian lira; N—Netherlands; f.—Netherlands guilder; U.S.—United States; $—U.S. dollar; CA—current account.

[2] The divergence indicator shows the movement of the exchange rate of each ERM currency against the (weighted) average movement of the other ERM currencies. The criterion used is the divergence of the actual daily rate of the ERM currency, expressed in ECUs, from its ECU central rate. Adjustments are made for those currencies contained in the ECU but not participating in the ERM and the wider margins observed by the Italian lira. A currency crossing a "threshold of convergence," set at 75 percent of the maximum divergence spread, raises the presumption that the authorities concerned will take corrective policy action. In practice, this provision has played only a limited role. For more details, see Ungerer (1983), p. 15.

Table 6. EMS: Bilateral Central Rates[1]

Currency Units	100 Belgian/ Luxembourg francs	100 Danish kroner	100 Deutsche mark	100 French francs	100 Italian lire	100 Irish pounds	100 Netherlands guilders
Belgian/Luxembourg francs							
Mar. 13, 1979		556.852	1,571.64	680.512	3.43668	5,954.71	1,450.26
Sept. 24, 1979		540.942	1,603.07	680.512	3.43668	5,954.71	1,450.26
Nov. 30, 1979		515.186	1,603.07	680.512	3.43668	5,954.71	1,450.26
Mar. 23, 1981		515.186	1,603.07	680.512	3.23048	5,954.71	1,450.26
Oct. 5, 1981		515.186	1,691.25	660.097	3.13355	5,954.71	1,530.03
Feb. 22, 1982		546.154	1,848.37	721.415	3.42466	6,507.92	1,672.16
June 14, 1982		546.154	1,926.93	679.941	3.33047	6,507.92	1,743.23
Mar. 21, 1983		551.536	2,002.85	653.144	3.19922	6,187.32	1,777.58
July 22, 1985		551.536	2,002.85	653.144	2.94831	6,187.32	1,777.58
Apr. 7, 1986		551.536	2,042.52	627.278	2.19120	6,126.06	1,812.78
Aug. 4, 1986		551.536	2,042.52	627.278	2.19120	5,635.98	1,812.78
Danish kroner							
Mar. 13, 1979	17.9581		282.237	122.207	0.617161	1,069.35	260.439
Sept. 24, 1979	18.4862		296.348	125.801	0.635312	1,100.81	268.098
Nov. 30, 1979	19.4105		311.165	132.091	0.667078	1,155.84	281.503
Mar. 23, 1981	19.4105		311.165	132.091	0.627052	1,155.84	281.503
Oct. 5, 1981	19.4105		328.279	128.128	0.60824	1,155.84	296.986
Feb. 22, 1982	18.3098		338.433	132.09	0.62705	1,191.59	306.171
June 14, 1982	18.3098		352.817	124.496	0.609804	1,191.59	319.183
Mar. 21, 1983	18.1312		363.141	118.423	0.580057	1,121.84	322.297
July 22, 1985	18.1312		363.141	118.423	0.534563	1,121.84	322.297
Apr. 7, 1986	18.1312		370.332	113.732	0.529268	1,110.72	328.676
Aug. 4, 1986	18.1312		370.332	113.732	0.529268	1,021.86	328.676
Deutsche mark							
Mar. 13, 1979	6.36277	35.4313		43.2995	0.218668	378.886	92.2767
Sept. 24, 1979	6.238	33.7441		42.4505	0.21438	371.457	90.4673
Nov. 30, 1979	6.238	32.1373		42.4505	0.21438	371.457	90.4673
Mar. 23, 1981	6.238	32.1373		42.4505	0.201518	371.457	90.4673
Oct. 5, 1981	5.9128	30.4619		39.0302	0.185281	352.09	90.4673
Feb. 22, 1982	5.41018	29.5479		39.0302	0.185281	353.09	90.4673
June 14, 1982	5.18961	28.3433		35.2863	0.172839	337.736	90.4673
Mar. 21, 1983	4.99288	27.5375		32.6107	0.159733	308.925	88.7526
July 22, 1985	4.99288	27.5375		32.6107	0.147205	308.925	88.7526
Apr. 7, 1986	4.8959	27.0028		30.7109	0.142917	299.926	88.7526
Aug. 4, 1986	4.8959	27.0028		30.7109	0.142917	275.934	88.7526
French francs							
Mar. 13, 1979	14.6948	81.8286	230.95		0.505013	875.034	213.113
Sept. 24, 1979	14.6948	79.4905	235.568		0.505013	875.034	213.113
Nov. 30, 1979	14.6948	75.7054	235.568		0.505013	875.034	213.113
Mar. 23, 1981	14.6948	75.7054	235.568		0.474714	875.034	213.113
Oct. 5, 1981	15.1493	78.047	256.212		0.474714	902.098	231.789
Feb. 22, 1982	13.8616	75.706	256.212		0.474714	902.098	231.789
June 14, 1982	14.7072	80.3239	283.396		0.489818	957.129	256.38
Mar. 21, 1983	15.3106	84.4432	306.648		0.489819	947.313	272.158
July 22, 1985	15.3106	84.4432	306.648		0.451402	947.313	272.158
Apr. 7, 1986	15.9419	87.9257	325.617		0.465362	976.610	288.991
Aug. 4, 1986	15.9419	87.9257	325.617		0.465362	898.480	288.991
Italian lire							
Mar. 13, 1979	2,909.79	16,303.3	45,731.4	19,801.5		173,270.0	42,199.5
Sept. 24, 1979	2,909.79	15,740.3	46,646.0	19,801.5		173,270.0	42,199.5
Nov. 30, 1979	2,909.79	14,990.7	46,646.0	19,801.5		173,270.0	42,199.5
Mar. 23, 1981	3,095.51	15,947.6	49,623.2	21,065.3		184,329.0	44,893.0
Oct. 5, 1981	3,191.26	16,440.9	53,972.2	21,065.3		190,031.0	48,827.2
Feb. 22, 1982	2,920.0	15,947.7	53,972.2	21,065.3		190,031.0	48,827.2
June 14, 1982	3,002.58	16,398.7	57,857.4	20,415.7		195,405.0	52,341.9
Mar. 21, 1983	3,125.76	17,239.7	62,604.3	20,415.7		193,401.0	55,563.0
July 22, 1985	3,191.77	18,706.9	67,932.5	22,153.2		209,860.8	60,291.5
Apr. 7, 1986	3,425.70	18,894.0	69,970.6	21,488.6		209,860.8	62,100.2
Aug. 4, 1986	3,425.70	18,894.0	69,970.6	21,488.6		193,071.0	62,100.2

Table 6 (*Concluded*).   EMS: Bilateral Central Rates[1]

Currency Units	100 Belgian/ Luxembourg francs	100 Danish kroner	100 Deutsche mark	100 French francs	100 Italian lire	100 Irish pounds	100 Netherlands guilders
Irish pounds							
Mar. 13, 1979	1.67934	9.35146	26.3932	11.4281	0.0577136		24.3548
Sept. 24, 1979	1.67934	9.08424	26.921	11.4281	0.0577136		24.3548
Nov. 30, 1979	1.67934	8.65169	26.921	11.4281	0.0577136		24.3548
Mar. 23, 1981	1.67934	8.65169	26.921	11.4281	0.0542508		24.3548
Oct. 5, 1981	1.67934	8.65169	28.4018	11.0853	0.052623		25.6944
Feb. 22, 1982	1.53659	8.39216	28.4018	11.0853	0.052623		25.6944
June 14, 1982	1.53659	8.39216	29.6090	10.4479	0.05111758		26.7864
Mar. 21, 1983	1.61621	8.91396	32.3703	10.5562	0.0517061		28.7295
July 22, 1985	1.61621	8.91396	32.3703	10.5562	0.0476508		28.7295
Apr. 7, 1986	1.63237	9.00315	33.3416	10.2395	0.0476508		29.5912
Aug. 4, 1986	1.77431	9.78604	36.2405	11.1299	0.0517943		32.1644
Netherlands guilders							
Mar. 13, 1979	6.89531	38.3967	108.37	46.9235	0.23697	410.597	
Sept. 24, 1979	6.89531	37.2998	110.537	46.9235	0.23697	410.597	
Nov. 30, 1979	6.89531	35.5237	110.537	46.9235	0.23697	410.597	
Mar. 23, 1981	6.89531	35.5237	110.537	46.9235	0.222752	410.597	
Oct. 5, 1981	6.53583	33.6716	110.537	43.1428	0.204804	389.19	
Feb. 22, 1982	5.98027	32.6615	110.537	43.1428	0.204804	389.19	
June 14, 1982	5.73646	31.3300	110.537	39.0045	0.191051	373.324	
Mar. 21, 1983	5.62561	31.0273	112.673	36.7434	0.179976	348.075	
July 22, 1985	5.62561	31.0273	112.673	36.7434	0.165861	348.075	
Apr. 7, 1986	5.51640	30.4251	112.673	34.6032	0.161030	337.938	
Aug. 4, 1986	5.51640	30.4251	112.673	34.6032	0.161030	310.903	

Sources: Commission of the European Communities; and Fund staff calculations.

[1] Expressed as the price of 100 units of the currency on top of the column in the currency in front of the row.

Table 7.   EMS Realignments: Percentage Changes in Bilateral Central Rates[1]

	Sept. 24, 1979	Nov. 30, 1979	Mar. 23, 1981	Oct. 5, 1981	Feb. 22, 1982	June 14, 1982	Mar. 21, 1983	July 22, 1985	April 7, 1986	Aug. 4, 1986
Belgian and Luxembourg francs					− 8.5		+ 1.5	+ 2.0	+ 1.0	
Danish krone	− 2.9	− 4.8			− 3.0		+ 2.5	+ 2.0	+ 1.0	
Deutsche mark	+ 2.0			+ 5.5		+ 4.25	+ 5.5	+ 2.0	+ 3.0	
French franc				− 3.0		− 5.75	− 2.5	+ 2.0	− 3.0	
Italian lira			− 6.0	− 3.0		− 2.75	− 2.5	− 6.0		
Irish pound							− 3.5	+ 2.0		− 8.0
Netherlands guilder				+ 5.5		+ 4.25	+ 3.5	+ 2.0	+ 3.0	

Sources: Commission of the European Communities; and Fund staff calculations.

[1] Calculated as the percentage change against the group of currencies whose bilateral parities remained unchanged in the realignment, except for the realignments (3/21/83, 7/20/85) in which all currencies were realigned—for this the percentages are shown as in the official communiqué.

Table 8. ECU Central Rates[1]

	Mar. 13, 1979	Sept. 24, 1979	Nov. 30, 1979	Mar. 23, 1981	Oct. 5, 1981	Feb. 22, 1982	June 14, 1982	Mar. 21, 1983	July 22,[2] 1985	Apr. 7, 1986	Aug. 4, 1986
Belgian/Luxembourg franc											
Units of national currency per ECU	39.4582	39.8456	39.7897	40.7985	40.7572	44.6963	44.9704	44.3662	44.8320	43.6761	43.1139
Percentage change from previous central rate		0.98	−0.14	2.54	−0.10	9.66	0.61	−1.34	−0.15	−2.58	−1.29
Percentage change from initial central rate		0.98	0.84	3.40	3.29	13.28	13.97	12.44	13.62	10.69	9.26
Danish krone											
Units of national currency per ECU	7.08592	7.36594	7.72336	7.91917	7.91117	8.18382	8.2340	8.04412	8.12857	7.91896	7.81701
Percentage change from previous central rate		3.95	4.85	2.54	−0.10	3.45	0.61	−2.31	−0.15	−2.58	−1.29
Percentage change from initial central rate		3.95	9.00	11.76	11.65	15.49	16.20	13.52	14.71	11.76	10.32
Deutsche mark											
Units of national currency per ECU	2.51064	2.48557	2.48208	2.54502	2.40989	2.41815	2.33379	2.21515	2.23840	2.13834	2.11083
Percentage change from previous central rate		−1.00	−0.1	2.54	−5.31	0.34	−3.48	−5.08	−0.15	−4.47	−1.29
Percentage change from initial central rate		−1.00	−0.1	1.37	−4.01	−3.68	−7.04	−11.77	−10.84	−14.83	−15.92
French franc											
Units of national currency per ECU	5.79831	5.85522	5.84700	5.99526	6.17443	6.19564	6.61387	6.79271	6.86402	6.9628	6.87316
Percentage change from previous central rate		0.98	−0.14	2.54	2.99	0.34	6.75	2.70	−0.15	1.44	−1.29
Percentage change from initial central rate		0.98	0.84	3.40	6.49	6.85	14.07	17.15	18.38	20.08	18.54
Italian lira											
Units of national currency per ECU	1,148.15	1,159.42	1,157.79	1,262.92	1,300.13	1,305.13	1,350.27	1,386.78	1,520.60	1,496.21	1,476.95
Percentage change from previous central rate		0.98	−0.14	9.1	2.99	0.34	3.46	2.70	8.34	−1.60	−1.29
Percentage change from initial central rate		0.98	0.84	10.00	13.28	13.67	17.60	20.78	32.44	30.31	28.64
Irish pound											
Units of national currency per ECU	0.662638	0.669141	0.668201	0.685145	0.684452	0.686799	0.691011	0.71705	0.724578	0.712956	0.764976
Percentage change from previous central rate		0.98	−0.14	2.54	−0.10	0.34	0.61	3.77	−0.15	−1.60	7.30
Percentage change from initial central rate		0.98	0.84	3.40	3.29	3.65	4.28	8.21	9.35	7.59	15.44
Netherlands guilder											
Units of national currency per ECU	2.72077	2.74748	2.74362	2.81318	2.66382	2.57971	2.49587	2.49587	2.52208	2.40935	2.37833
Percentage change from previous central rate		0.98	−0.14	2.54	−5.31	0.34	−3.49	−3.25	−0.15	−4.47	−1.29
Percentage change from initial central rate		0.98	0.84	3.40	−2.09	−1.76	−5.18	−8.27	−7.30	−11.45	−12.59

Source: Commission of the European Communities.
[1] The change of any central rate expressed in terms of ECUs implies a simultaneous change of all other ECU central rates since the ECU is made up of a basket of currencies. Positive sign indicates depreciation relative to the ECU.
[2] Percentage change from central rate as of May 1983, when the notional central rate of the pound sterling was revalued and the other central rates devalued as part of a package to arrive at new common agricultural prices. No change in bilateral central rates and intervention limits of participating currencies occurred at this time.

Table 9. Interest Differentials for Three-Month Deposits, 1979–86[1]

		France		Germany	
		Uncovered[2]	Covered[3]	Uncovered[2]	Covered[3]
1979	I	−2.60	1.03	−6.81	−1.54
	II	−1.39	−0.46	5.17	−1.01
	III	0.25	1.38	5.09	0.07
	IV	−1.66	0.53	−6.15	−0.49
1980	I	−2.57	3.19	−7.46	2.00
	II	−0.50	−3.05	−3.85	−3.81
	III	0.62	2.38	−2.60	2.32
	IV	−5.45	0.40	−7.92	0.25
1981	I	−4.92	−2.82	−5.71	−3.47
	II	0.63	0.60	−4.75	0.59
	III	5.83	5.18	−6.04	−0.61
	IV	3.63	3.63	−3.42	−0.26
1982	I	1.69	0.92	−5.64	0.35
	II	7.02	7.90	−6.23	0.57
	III	5.14	2.62	−4.16	−0.42
	IV	10.81	7.30	−2.63	0.65
1983	I	14.20	11.69	−4.03	0.34
	II	4.64	1.89	−4.22	0.17
	III	4.65	1.75	−4.66	−1.00
	IV	3.73	1.36	−3.57	0.36
1984	I	4.70	2.80	−4.41	0.37
	II	1.62	1.60	−5.61	0.74
	III	−0.16	0.22	−6.21	−0.75
	IV	1.16	−0.85	−4.19	−1.27
1985	I	1.99	0.25	−2.92	0.05
	II	2.28	−0.21	−2.53	−0.34
	III	2.82	0.58	−3.32	0.11
	IV	2.38	1.38	−3.33	−0.36
1986	I	5.59	4.72	−3.44	−0.76

Source: International Monetary Fund, *International Financial Statistics,* various issues.

[1] London Interbank offered rates on three-month deposits.

[2] London Interbank offered rate minus corresponding London Interbank offer rate on U.S. dollar deposits.

[3] Uncovered interest rate differential plus discount or premium on three-month forward exchange rates against the U.S. dollar.

Table 10. EMS: Economic Measures in Connection with Realignments

Realignment Date	Realignment Wording Based on Official Communiqué	Major Measures in			
		Belgium	Denmark	France	Italy
September 24, 1979	Shift in cross-rate between the deutsche mark and the Danish krone of 5 percent. Shift in cross-rate between the deutsche mark and other EMS currencies of 2 percent.	—	—	—	—
November 30, 1979	Devaluation of the Danish krone by 5 percent against other EMS currencies (no communiqué).	—	• Energy component removed from wage-regulating index • Short-term price and wage freeze measures • Increases in direct personal wealth and corporate taxes.	—	—
March 23, 1981	Devaluation of Italian lira by 6 percent against other EMS currencies.	—	—	—	• Discount rate up 2½ percent to 19 percent • Government spending cut plans.
October 5, 1981	Revaluation of the deutsche mark and the Netherlands guilder by 5.5 percent against the Danish krone, the Belgian franc, the Luxembourg franc, and the Irish pound. Devaluation of the French franc and the Italian lira by 3 percent against the Danish krone, the Belgian franc, and the Irish pound.	—	—	• Temporary price and profit freeze • Incomes policy aiming at maintenance of average income purchasing power, narrowing of income range • F 10.15 billion government expenditure in suspense.	—
February 22, 1982	Devaluation of the Belgian franc and the Luxembourg franc by 8.5 percent and the Danish krone by 3 percent against other EMS currencies.	• Temporary freeze of wages and longer-run measures to impede complete wage indexation • Temporary price freeze • Reduction in corporate tax burden • Measures to stimulate the stock market.	—	—	—
June 14, 1982	Change in bilateral rates: between the French franc, and the deutsche mark, f.: 10 percent; between the Italian lira and the deutsche mark, f.: 7 percent; between the	—	—	• Temporary freeze of wages, prices, rents, and dividends (except minimum wage) to be followed up by agreements on price and dividend	• Announcement of budgetary austerity measures, June 23.

Table 10 (*Concluded*).   **EMS: Economic Measures in Connection with Realignments**

Realignment Date	Realignment Wording Based on Official Communiqué	Major Measures in			
		Belgium	Denmark	France	Italy
	Danish krone, the Belgian franc, the Luxembourg franc, the Irish pound, and the deutsche mark, f.: 4.25 percent.			behavior and indexation practices for wages • Revision of 1983 budget to restrict deficit to FF 120 billion (3 percent of gross national product).	
March 21, 1983	Change in central rates Deutsche mark +5.5 Netherlands guilder +3.5 Danish krone +2.5 Belgian franc +1.5 Luxembourg franc +1.5 French franc −2.5 Italian lira −2.5 Irish pound −3.5	—	—	• Package of restrictive measures in budgetary, monetary, and foreign exchange fields.	—
July 20, 1985	Change in central rates Irish pound +2 French franc +2 Danish krone +2 Netherlands guilder +2 Deutsche mark +2 Belgian franc +2 Luxembourg franc +2 Italian lira −6	—	—	—	• Announcement of a package of revenue-raising measures aiming at containing an increase in the fiscal deficit over the target for 1985 • Modification of the wage indexation mechanism (scala mobile).
April 6, 1986	Change in central rates Deutsche mark +3 Netherlands guilder +3 Belgian franc +1 Luxembourg franc +1 Danish krone +1 Irish pound 0 Italian lira 0 French franc −3	—	—	• Steps to slow nominal wage growth and to reduce the government budget deficit. The noninterest component of the deficit is to be eliminated in the course of the next three years. • The target to contain the growth of M3 below 5 percent in 1986 was reasserted. • Relaxation of exchange controls.	—
August 2, 1986	Devaluation of the Irish pound by 8 percent vis-à-vis all other participating currencies.	—	—	—	—

Sources: Commission of the European Communities; and Fund staff estimates.

Table 11.   Indicators of Competitiveness in Manufacturing as Measured by Unit Labor Costs Adjusted for Exchange Rate Changes in Relation to EMS Partner Countries[1]

(1979 I = 100)

	Belgium	Denmark[2]	France	Germany, Fed. Rep. of	Ireland	Italy	Netherlands
1979	97.8	97.0	101.2	99.0	106.4	104.3	95.9
1980	93.1	86.8	106.3	98.9	121.6	103.5	92.4
1981	89.6	87.7	107.8	97.2	127.2	109.7	87.4
1982	77.3	85.6	104.4	100.0	134.3	116.3	91.0
1983	74.0	86.1	100.9	99.8	122.6	125.9	88.9
1984	74.4	83.7	103.0	100.5	115.8	125.6	82.8
1985	77.0	87.8	105.4	99.2	117.4	123.0	81.1
1982 I	83.9	87.7	107.9	97.0	132.1	112.8	89.5
1982 II	76.2	86.8	108.4	98.9	136.8	114.2	89.4
1982 III	74.8	85.2	101.2	102.7	136.2	117.5	91.2
1982 IV	74.1	82.6	100.1	101.6	132.2	120.5	94.0
1983 I	74.2	87.1	102.6	98.8	123.6	123.5	91.3
1983 II	74.4	86.3	99.2	100.7	123.4	125.8	90.0
1983 III	74.1	85.5	100.8	100.0	123.5	126.7	87.3
1983 IV	73.2	85.4	101.1	99.9	120.0	127.4	87.0
1984 I	72.3	83.2	101.6	103.6	119.6	123.3	83.0
1984 II	74.1	84.2	103.3	100.3	112.9	125.8	82.6
1984 III	75.6	83.5	103.0	98.7	118.8	127.7	83.5
1984 IV	75.7	83.8	104.0	99.5	112.0	125.7	82.0
1985 I	77.5	88.1	105.1	97.3	112.7	127.0	80.7
1985 II	77.6	87.6	105.6	98.5	117.1	124.0	80.7
1985 III	76.9	87.8	105.5	99.6	121.5	122.1	80.8
1985 IV	76.2	87.5	105.5	101.4	118.1	118.9	82.0
1986 I	77.6	91.3	105.4	103.9	115.3	115.4	78.4

Sources: International Monetary Fund, *International Financial Statistics,* various issues; and Fund staff calculations.

[1] Unit labor costs against the weighted average of unit labor costs of the other countries participating in the EMS exchange rate mechanism (in common currency).

[2] Unit labor costs for Denmark based on sales in manufacturing rather than output.

Table 12. Indicators of Competitiveness in Manufacturing as Measured by Unit Labor Costs Adjusted for Exchange Rate Changes in Relation to 16 Industrial Partner Countries[1]

(1979 I = 100)

	Belgium	Denmark[2]	France	Germany, Fed. Rep. of	Ireland	Italy	Netherlands
1979	97.0	96.0	100.3	98.6	102.7	103.4	95.1
1980	90.8	83.6	103.0	96.8	107.6	101.4	89.6
1981	83.0	78.6	97.9	88.6	103.3	100.8	80.0
1982	71.2	77.4	94.2	89.6	109.3	105.3	82.3
1983	68.6	79.8	92.3	90.2	103.1	114.0	81.0
1984	67.4	74.7	91.3	87.6	93.9	110.8	73.5
1985	68.9	76.9	91.9	85.4	92.5	107.2	71.1
1982 I	77.3	78.7	97.1	87.5	107.4	102.5	81.2
1982 II	70.1	77.5	96.9	88.4	110.5	103.3	80.5
1982 III	68.9	76.6	91.4	91.3	110.6	106.1	82.3
1982 IV	68.6	76.6	91.2	91.4	108.7	109.2	85.3
1983 I	70.2	82.7	95.7	91.6	108.2	114.4	84.8
1983 II	69.2	80.6	91.3	91.3	103.9	114.4	82.3
1983 III	68.2	78.4	91.5	89.4	102.1	113.8	78.9
1983 IV	66.8	77.5	90.8	88.3	98.2	113.2	77.9
1984 I	66.0	75.3	90.9	90.6	97.8	109.9	74.3
1984 II	67.9	76.1	92.8	88.8	93.1	112.5	74.3
1984 III	68.1	73.8	90.8	85.8	95.5	111.8	73.7
1984 IV	67.6	73.4	90.5	85.3	89.1	109.1	71.8
1985 I	68.8	76.7	90.5	83.1	89.6	109.1	70.2
1985 II	68.8	76.1	91.2	84.1	91.0	107.1	70.2
1985 III	68.7	76.6	92.0	85.6	94.4	106.6	70.8
1985 IV	69.4	78.0	94.0	88.8	95.1	106.2	73.3
1986 I	72.1	83.8	96.3	92.9	97.3	105.8	72.0

Sources: International Monetary Fund, *International Financial Statistics,* various issues; and Fund staff calculations.

[1] Unit labor costs against the weighted average of unit labor costs of 16 industrial partner countries. Weights are those used to calculate relative unit labor costs for 17 industrial countries as published in *International Financial Statistics*.

[2] Unit labor costs for Denmark based on sales in manufacturing rather than output.

Table 13.   Indicators of Competitiveness as Measured by Consumer Prices Adjusted for Exchange Rate Changes in Relation to EMS Partner Countries[1]

(1979 I = 100)

	Belgium	Denmark	France	Germany, Fed. Rep. of	Ireland	Italy	Netherlands
1979	97.8	99.4	101.0	98.8	103.2	103.4	98.2
1980	94.9	95.5	105.1	93.4	111.7	111.2	96.5
1981	92.6	97.8	107.3	91.2	121.5	114.3	95.0
1982	85.1	95.3	103.1	94.5	130.8	117.3	98.5
1983	84.1	95.0	98.3	95.4	129.8	124.2	97.2
1984	85.1	95.9	98.7	93.1	131.8	128.2	95.8
1985	86.5	98.2	101.8	90.7	135.2	127.7	94.2
1982 I	88.0	96.0	106.4	92.5	126.9	115.0	97.3
1982 II	83.5	95.1	106.4	94.3	131.7	114.6	97.7
1982 III	84.8	94.8	100.0	95.7	133.2	118.9	99.4
1982 IV	84.1	95.3	99.5	95.5	131.6	120.6	99.7
1983 I	84.0	94.6	100.0	94.9	130.6	122.3	97.7
1983 II	84.2	95.5	97.4	96.2	128.7	123.9	96.9
1983 III	84.5	94.5	97.9	95.3	130.1	124.7	96.9
1983 IV	83.8	95.3	97.7	95.0	129.9	126.0	97.1
1984 I	84.2	95.0	97.6	94.8	130.7	126.6	96.5
1984 II	84.7	95.1	98.3	93.8	131.4	127.6	96.3
1984 III	85.7	96.1	99.2	92.3	132.5	128.7	95.3
1984 IV	85.6	97.4	99.6	91.6	132.8	129.7	95.2
1985 I	86.4	98.1	99.5	90.9	133.6	131.5	93.7
1985 II	86.4	98.4	101.3	90.5	134.9	129.2	94.0
1985 III	86.8	98.0	103.2	90.8	137.0	125.0	94.6
1985 IV	86.4	98.2	103.4	90.8	135.5	125.1	94.7
1986 I	86.1	96.6	102.7	90.8	135.0	126.7	94.2

Sources: International Monetary Fund, *International Financial Statistics,* various issues; and Fund staff calculations.

[1] Consumer prices against the weighted average of consumer prices of the other countries participating in the EMS exchange rate mechanism (in common currency).

Table 14.   Indicators of Competitiveness as Measured by Consumer Prices Adjusted for Exchange Rate Changes in Relation to 16 Industrial Partner Countries[1]

(1979 I = 100)

	Belgium	Denmark	France	Germany, Fed. Rep. of	Ireland	Italy	Netherlands
1979	97.2	98.6	100.3	98.7	100.0	102.8	97.5
1980	92.6	91.5	102.4	92.7	100.7	108.5	93.6
1981	85.7	86.7	97.4	84.2	99.4	104.3	86.5
1982	78.1	84.9	92.7	85.3	106.1	105.3	88.6
1983	77.1	85.8	88.9	85.6	107.5	110.7	87.4
1984	76.2	83.8	86.8	81.4	106.7	110.7	84.1
1985	76.9	84.6	88.5	79.0	107.8	109.5	82.1
1982 I	81.1	85.3	96.0	84.4	103.8	104.1	88.1
1982 II	76.8	84.3	95.6	85.3	107.0	103.5	88.0
1982 III	77.1	83.3	89.3	85.2	106.4	105.6	88.6
1982 IV	77.2	86.6	89.9	86.2	107.4	108.0	89.8
1983 I	78.6	88.1	92.5	87.8	112.8	111.9	90.0
1983 II	77.4	86.8	88.6	86.7	107.0	111.0	87.6
1983 III	76.6	84.1	87.5	84.5	105.3	109.8	86.2
1983 IV	75.6	84.3	86.9	83.6	105.0	110.1	85.9
1984 I	76.0	83.8	86.7	83.3	106.2	110.4	85.3
1984 II	76.5	83.9	87.3	82.7	107.4	111.4	85.3
1984 III	76.5	83.4	86.8	80.4	106.6	110.7	83.3
1984 IV	75.9	83.9	86.2	79.1	106.5	110.4	82.6
1985 I	76.0	83.7	85.4	77.9	106.8	110.8	80.7
1985 II	76.0	83.8	87.0	77.9	105.3	109.4	80.9
1985 III	77.2	84.4	89.6	79.2	107.9	107.7	82.4
1985 IV	78.3	86.4	91.8	80.9	111.0	110.0	84.2
1986 I	80.0	87.5	93.8	83.4	116.7	114.3	86.0

Source: International Monetary Fund, *International Financial Statistics*, various issues; and Fund staff calculations.

[1] Consumer prices against the weighted average of consumer prices of 16 industrial countries. Weights are those used to calculate relative consumer prices for 17 industrial countries as published in *International Financial Statistics*.

Table 15.   Currencies for which Measure of Variability[1] Rose from 1974–78 to 1979–85, by Table and Country Group

Table	ERM Countries	Non-ERM Countries
16	None	Japan, Sweden, United Kingdom, United States
17	None	Canada, Japan, Sweden, United Kingdom, United States
18	None	Canada, Japan, Norway, Sweden, United Kingdom, United States
19	None	Japan, Sweden, United Kingdom, United States
20	None	Canada, Japan, Sweden, United Kingdom, United States
21	None	Canada, Japan, Norway, Sweden, United Kingdom, United States
22	All seven	Austria, Japan, Norway, Sweden, United Kingdom, United States
23	All seven	All eight
24	All but Italy	Austria, Japan, Switzerland, United Kingdom, United States
25	All seven	Austria, Japan, Norway, Sweden, United Kingdom, United States
26	All seven	All eight
27	All seven	Austria, Japan, United Kingdom, United States
28	Denmark, France	Austria, Japan, United Kingdom, United States
29	Denmark	Austria, Japan, United Kingdom, United States

Source: Tables 16–29.

[1] Arithmetic average of variability in each of the years within the relevant period.

Table 16. Variability of Bilateral Nominal Exchange Rates Against ERM Currencies, 1974–85[1]

	1974	1975	1976	1977	1978	1979	1980	1981	1982	1983	1984	1985	Average 1974–78	Average 1979–85
Belgium	21.2	17.8	34.5	12.2	15.8	8.2	6.3	17.1	36.0	12.3	6.5	9.2	20.3	13.6
Denmark	24.5	14.6	41.3	28.1	16.3	26.3	7.8	17.7	19.4	11.7	7.6	13.5	25.0	14.8
France	32.8	26.6	57.5	15.0	26.3	9.2	7.5	21.8	35.4	19.7	3.4	14.5	31.6	15.9
Germany, Fed. Rep. of	28.9	20.8	52.9	21.8	21.8	12.2	6.6	28.0	32.1	18.7	3.8	12.9	29.2	16.3
Ireland	26.5	33.4	73.2	16.6	30.1	12.1	6.9	15.5	20.8	14.0	5.9	10.0	36.0	12.2
Italy	42.0	18.7	70.0	20.4	28.7	14.1	11.6	27.9	24.2	14.4	5.7	36.9	36.0	19.3
Netherlands	21.7	15.0	39.4	13.2	16.0	9.3	7.5	22.8	26.4	11.9	3.4	11.1	21.1	13.2
Average ERM[2]	**28.2**	**21.0**	**52.7**	**18.2**	**22.1**	**13.0**	**7.7**	**21.5**	**27.7**	**14.7**	**5.2**	**15.4**	*28.4*	*15.1*
Austria	26.5	12.4	34.8	13.6	14.0	16.9	6.1	21.0	18.9	11.2	3.3	8.7	20.3	12.3
Canada	30.4	42.5	45.3	42.1	60.3	28.1	29.9	66.5	48.6	56.0	45.9	89.3	44.1	52.0
Japan	41.9	31.7	39.3	40.3	69.4	78.9	88.2	32.8	26.9	56.3	27.5	26.3	44.5	48.1
Norway	20.2	16.1	34.0	28.1	28.1	12.4	24.3	26.7	41.0	34.3	10.3	20.0	25.3	24.2
Sweden	19.9	14.9	33.7	65.6	17.1	13.7	22.3	48.7	67.3	29.8	17.3	22.0	30.2	31.6
Switzerland	45.8	21.5	45.0	49.0	59.0	9.8	17.0	65.7	24.3	29.2	13.9	21.4	44.0	25.9
United Kingdom	24.0	30.0	67.2	14.6	27.4	35.3	52.3	44.6	29.5	44.2	19.6	38.8	32.7	37.8
United States	32.7	44.5	38.4	19.1	38.6	23.0	40.9	71.2	52.4	58.8	58.6	84.9	34.7	55.7
Average non-ERM[2]	**30.2**	**26.7**	**42.2**	**34.0**	**39.3**	**27.3**	**35.1**	**47.1**	**38.6**	**40.0**	**24.5**	**38.9**	*34.5*	*35.9*
Average European non-ERM[2]	**27.3**	**19.0**	**42.9**	**34.2**	**29.1**	**17.6**	**24.4**	**41.3**	**36.2**	**29.7**	**12.9**	**22.2**	*30.5*	*26.3*

Sources: International Monetary Fund, *International Financial Statistics,* various issues; and Fund staff calculations.

[1] Weighted average (multilateral exchange rate model (MERM) weights) of variability of bilateral nominal exchange rates against EMS currencies, with variability measured by coefficient of variation (multiplied by 1,000) of average monthly bilateral exchange rates.

[2] Unweighted average.

Table 17. Variability of Log Changes of Bilateral Nominal Exchange Rates Against ERM Currencies, 1974–85[1]

	1974	1975	1976	1977	1978	1979	1980	1981	1982	1983	1984	1985	Average 1974–78	Average 1979–85
Belgium	13.6	6.9	13.6	8.0	10.7	4.8	3.9	8.5	20.3	6.4	3.3	3.9	10.6	7.3
Denmark	14.1	7.3	19.2	11.5	11.8	13.6	4.1	8.3	9.0	8.3	4.5	4.8	12.8	7.5
France	19.9	11.0	23.5	8.6	21.1	5.1	5.2	11.1	14.0	9.5	3.1	5.3	16.8	7.6
Germany, Fed. Rep. of	18.9	8.8	20.8	10.4	14.6	5.4	4.1	11.9	10.0	8.7	3.8	5.0	14.7	7.0
Ireland	14.4	14.9	29.9	12.2	20.5	8.5	4.8	7.9	9.8	6.9	4.7	4.5	18.4	6.7
Italy	17.4	10.6	40.6	11.3	16.3	8.7	5.9	12.8	9.2	8.5	5.7	10.6	19.3	8.8
Netherlands	12.5	7.5	16.0	8.4	11.1	5.7	3.7	10.8	9.8	5.8	2.9	4.3	11.1	6.1
Average ERM[2]	**15.8**	**9.6**	**23.4**	**10.1**	**15.1**	**7.4**	**4.5**	**10.2**	**11.7**	**7.8**	**4.0**	**5.5**	*14.8*	*7.3*
Austria	13.1	5.7	14.0	7.2	9.6	6.7	3.1	8.6	6.1	5.7	2.6	3.4	9.9	5.2
Canada	17.5	24.2	25.3	13.2	32.1	18.4	20.2	29.9	30.8	14.5	30.5	26.7	22.5	24.4
Japan	19.7	19.2	19.2	16.7	30.6	20.0	27.4	30.7	19.7	11.4	18.7	24.1	21.1	21.7
Norway	12.9	9.2	14.6	12.6	17.3	8.7	11.6	18.7	21.1	11.5	9.8	8.9	13.3	12.9
Sweden	13.1	7.8	14.2	24.5	13.5	8.2	8.6	31.4	41.6	9.2	10.6	10.9	14.6	17.2
Switzerland	18.8	11.6	20.0	16.4	35.8	9.3	11.1	20.2	16.5	12.3	10.7	11.3	20.5	13.1
United Kingdom	13.3	13.5	27.4	11.1	18.6	22.1	13.1	27.7	23.9	24.1	12.0	23.7	16.8	20.9
United States	19.9	22.5	17.2	10.8	23.7	14.5	27.7	36.9	31.5	16.0	30.2	35.2	18.8	27.4
Average non-ERM[2]	**16.0**	**14.2**	**19.0**	**14.1**	**22.6**	**13.5**	**15.4**	**25.5**	**23.9**	**13.1**	**15.6**	**18.0**	*17.2*	*17.9*
Average European non-ERM[2]	**14.2**	**9.6**	**18.0**	**14.4**	**18.9**	**11.0**	**9.5**	**21.3**	**21.8**	**12.5**	**9.1**	**11.6**	*15.0*	*13.9*

Sources: International Monetary Fund, *International Financial Statistics,* various issues; and Fund staff calculations.

[1] Weighted average (MERM weights) of variability of bilateral nominal exchange rates against ERM currencies, with variability measured by the standard deviation (multiplied by 1,000) of changes in the natural logarithm of average monthly bilateral exchange rates.

[2] Unweighted average.

Table 18. Variability of Log Changes of Nominal Effective Exchange Rates Against ERM Currencies, 1974–85[1]

	1974	1975	1976	1977	1978	1979	1980	1981	1982	1983	1984	1985	Average 1974–78	Average 1979–85	F probabilities [2]
Belgium	9.4	4.4	8.9	5.8	9.0	3.4	2.9	4.3	19.4	4.3	2.4	2.6	7.5	5.6	0.832
Denmark	10.2	4.1	14.5	9.7	7.4	13.0	2.8	3.7	5.5	7.0	3.5	3.1	9.2	5.5	—
France	18.1	9.9	16.8	5.1	19.8	3.2	4.7	8.6	12.7	8.6	1.2	3.9	13.9	6.1	—
Germany, Fed. Rep. of	17.4	6.6	17.2	9.2	12.4	4.1	2.6	10.5	6.5	7.8	3.5	3.8	12.6	5.5	—
Ireland	9.3	14.1	25.5	10.7	17.8	7.2	4.0	3.6	7.3	5.5	4.0	3.6	15.5	5.0	—
Italy	13.3	9.2	39.9	10.7	12.0	8.3	5.6	11.6	6.6	6.7	5.6	10.5	17.0	7.8	—
Netherlands	6.9	5.3	9.1	6.0	9.0	4.3	2.3	9.3	7.1	2.1	2.0	3.4	7.3	4.4	0.001
Average ERM[3]	**12.1**	**7.7**	**18.9**	**8.2**	**12.5**	**6.2**	**3.5**	**7.4**	**9.3**	**6.0**	**3.2**	**4.4**	**11.8**	**5.7**	n/a
Austria	9.5	3.3	8.6	5.4	5.6	5.7	1.9	7.4	3.7	4.7	2.0	2.4	6.5	3.9	—
Canada	13.5	23.7	20.6	11.8	30.5	17.9	20.0	29.2	30.0	13.5	30.4	26.4	20.0	23.9	0.096
Japan	16.2	18.6	14.0	15.6	29.0	19.5	27.2	30.0	18.2	10.1	18.6	23.8	18.7	21.1	0.095
Norway	7.4	7.3	9.1	11.1	13.8	7.1	11.2	17.3	20.1	10.3	9.4	7.8	9.7	11.9	0.075
Sweden	8.3	5.3	6.9	23.7	8.8	6.3	8.0	30.7	41.0	7.7	10.3	10.1	10.6	16.3	0.001
Switzerland	15.4	10.3	14.0	15.4	34.2	8.3	10.8	19.2	15.1	11.2	10.4	10.9	17.9	12.3	0.006
United Kingdom	8.5	12.8	23.2	9.8	16.1	21.8	12.8	26.8	22.9	23.6	11.7	23.4	14.1	20.4	0.003
United States	16.9	22.0	9.9	10.1	21.4	13.8	27.6	36.3	30.8	15.2	30.1	34.9	16.0	27.0	—
Average non-ERM[3]	**12.0**	**12.9**	**13.3**	**12.9**	**19.9**	**12.5**	**14.9**	**24.6**	**22.7**	**12.0**	**15.4**	**17.4**	**14.2**	**17.1**	n/a
Average European non-ERM[3]	**9.8**	**7.8**	**12.3**	**13.1**	**15.7**	**9.8**	**8.9**	**20.3**	**20.6**	**11.5**	**8.8**	**10.9**	**11.7**	**13.0**	n/a

Sources: International Monetary Fund, *International Financial Statistics,* various issues; and Fund staff calculations.

[1] Variability of weighted average (MERM weights) of bilateral nominal exchange rates against ERM currencies, with variability measured by the standard deviation (multiplied by 1,000) of changes in the natural logarithm of the effective exchange rate index.

[2] Probability that the variance of the change in the natural logarithm of the effective exchange rate index in period 1 (January 1974 to February 1979) is equal to corresponding variance in period 2 (March 1979 to December 1985), where the effective exchange rate index is a weighted average of the given country's exchange rate with respect to the ERM currencies; MERM weights were used.

[3] Unweighted average.

Table 19. Variability of Bilateral Real Exchange Rates Against ERM Currencies, 1974–85[1]

	1974	1975	1976	1977	1978	1979	1980	1981	1982	1983	1984	1985	Average 1974–78	Average 1979–85
Belgium	31.6	19.4	31.4	8.5	19.0	17.2	14.1	10.9	34.7	7.2	9.5	8.4	*22.0*	*14.6*
Denmark	28.9	24.3	43.7	14.6	18.5	22.1	15.0	12.6	18.4	9.3	10.3	10.1	*26.0*	*14.0*
France	29.3	30.9	48.1	10.2	32.9	15.7	19.5	11.9	38.1	11.9	10.0	17.5	*30.3*	*17.8*
Germany, Fed. Rep. of	36.8	32.2	37.2	11.7	22.4	16.6	25.6	13.2	23.3	9.4	14.7	11.9	*28.0*	*16.4*
Ireland	25.5	29.3	46.1	11.8	25.4	22.1	16.8	15.5	20.8	11.6	9.8	13.5	*27.6*	*15.7*
Italy	25.1	25.1	48.4	10.9	21.4	22.8	23.8	12.6	25.7	12.9	11.2	23.3	*26.2*	*18.9*
Netherlands	22.6	19.9	35.6	11.3	16.3	19.3	14.9	15.3	18.6	7.3	10.4	9.8	*21.1*	*13.6*
Average ERM[2]	**28.6**	**25.9**	**41.5**	**11.3**	**22.3**	**19.4**	**18.5**	**13.1**	**25.7**	**9.9**	**10.9**	**13.5**	*25.9*	*15.9*
Austria	24.7	18.9	29.2	8.4	15.7	14.2	15.3	9.9	14.9	6.9	9.1	8.4	*19.4*	*11.3*
Canada	32.3	50.1	38.6	38.7	57.2	32.4	32.8	67.9	49.5	51.7	43.2	88.2	*43.4*	*52.2*
Japan	31.1	34.3	35.2	34.8	66.3	85.1	83.3	26.7	26.2	45.1	25.6	26.3	*40.3*	*45.5*
Norway	21.1	19.3	29.6	27.2	26.5	20.7	31.7	24.7	40.0	32.0	11.8	14.5	*24.8*	*25.1*
Sweden	21.7	18.9	28.5	52.8	18.9	14.4	29.5	53.6	67.0	32.1	22.9	16.6	*28.2*	*33.7*
Switzerland	38.3	23.5	32.7	36.2	47.8	19.3	18.2	52.3	24.5	17.0	19.5	16.2	*35.7*	*23.9*
United Kingdom	22.7	23.1	54.5	16.1	24.4	56.6	60.6	43.8	29.9	43.0	18.9	45.9	*28.1*	*42.7*
United States	34.6	45.4	30.8	21.6	32.9	21.2	43.8	69.2	46.7	52.6	57.4	83.5	*33.1*	*53.5*
Average non-ERM[2]	**28.3**	**29.2**	**34.9**	**29.5**	**36.2**	**33.0**	**39.4**	**43.5**	**37.3**	**35.1**	**26.0**	**37.5**	*31.6*	*36.0*
Average European non-ERM[2]	**25.7**	**20.7**	**34.9**	**28.1**	**26.7**	**25.0**	**31.1**	**36.9**	**35.3**	**26.2**	**16.4**	**20.3**	*27.2*	*27.3*

Sources: International Monetary Fund, *International Financial Statistics,* various issues; and Fund staff calculations.

[1] Weighted average (MERM weights) of variability of bilateral real exchange rates (nominal exchange rates adjusted for relative consumer price movements—wholesale prices for Ireland) against ERM currencies, with variability measured by the coefficient of variation (multiplied by 1,000) of average monthly bilateral exchange rates.

[2] Unweighted average.

Table 20. Variability of Log Changes of Bilateral Real Exchange Rates Against ERM Currencies, 1974–85[1]

	1974	1975	1976	1977	1978	1979	1980	1981	1982	1983	1984	1985	Average 1974–78	Average 1979–85
Belgium	14.8	8.5	14.0	9.5	12.3	6.2	5.1	8.4	22.9	6.6	4.5	5.3	*11.8*	*8.4*
Denmark	15.6	13.7	24.7	15.4	14.7	17.3	6.5	9.6	10.7	9.4	5.9	5.9	*16.8*	*9.3*
France	20.3	10.9	21.9	10.4	22.7	5.7	7.9	11.9	16.6	7.6	3.8	6.6	*17.2*	*8.6*
Germany, Fed. Rep. of	20.7	9.7	20.3	12.1	15.8	6.0	6.8	11.9	12.3	7.5	4.5	6.0	*15.7*	*7.9*
Ireland	14.8	23.2	28.4	12.2	21.2	13.3	12.3	11.6	12.1	9.0	7.9	14.5	*20.0*	*11.5*
Italy	20.2	10.9	36.2	13.4	17.4	8.2	7.9	13.2	11.8	7.7	5.3	11.9	*19.6*	*9.4*
Netherlands	13.5	10.3	18.0	10.9	12.1	7.0	6.1	11.4	11.6	5.4	4.2	5.5	*12.9*	*7.3*
Average ERM[2]	**17.1**	**12.5**	**23.4**	**12.0**	**16.6**	**9.1**	**7.5**	**11.1**	**14.0**	**7.6**	**5.2**	**8.0**	*16.3*	*8.9*
Austria	14.5	8.0	15.1	9.5	11.0	7.3	6.2	10.2	8.8	6.6	5.7	5.1	*11.6*	*7.2*
Canada	18.7	26.4	24.6	12.6	34.5	19.5	20.3	30.9	31.3	15.4	30.0	26.6	*23.3*	*24.9*
Japan	23.1	20.4	20.9	16.6	32.0	20.9	30.0	29.0	18.7	13.4	22.9	25.3	*22.6*	*22.9*
Norway	13.5	11.8	15.2	14.2	17.3	9.3	12.4	18.1	24.0	9.7	10.1	10.8	*14.4*	*13.5*
Sweden	15.3	9.9	15.7	25.4	14.6	9.1	12.4	32.8	40.0	9.9	14.6	12.2	*16.2*	*18.7*
Switzerland	21.3	12.5	18.7	18.7	36.0	11.7	12.8	19.2	15.2	11.9	11.0	10.7	*21.4*	*13.2*
United Kingdom	15.9	12.7	27.0	12.8	19.1	29.6	14.9	29.8	24.2	25.9	13.7	27.1	*17.5*	*23.6*
United States	21.3	24.3	17.2	11.6	24.0	15.3	28.5	38.2	33.2	16.3	31.2	34.8	*19.7*	*28.2*
Average non-ERM[2]	**17.9**	**15.7**	**19.3**	**15.2**	**23.6**	**15.3**	**17.2**	**26.0**	**24.4**	**13.6**	**17.4**	**19.2**	*18.3*	*19.0*
Average European non-ERM[2]	**16.1**	**11.0**	**18.3**	**16.1**	**19.6**	**13.4**	**11.7**	**22.0**	**22.4**	**12.8**	**11.0**	**13.2**	*16.2*	*15.2*

Sources: International Monetary Fund, *International Financial Statistics,* various issues; and Fund staff calculations.

[1] Weighted average (MERM weights) of variability of bilateral real exchange rates (nominal exchange rates adjusted for relative consumer price movements—wholesale prices for Ireland) against ERM currencies, with variability measured by the standard deviation (multiplied by 1,000) of changes in the natural logarithm of average monthly bilateral exchange rates.

[2] Unweighted average.

Table 21.   Variability of Log Changes of Real Effective Exchange Rates Against ERM Currencies, 1974–85[1]

	1974	1975	1976	1977	1978	1979	1980	1981	1982	1983	1984	1985	Average 1974–78	Average 1979–85	F probabilities[2]
Belgium	9.6	5.8	7.2	6.7	9.9	5.0	2.8	3.6	21.7	5.1	3.8	4.3	*7.9*	*6.6*	0.540
Denmark	10.8	11.9	20.7	13.6	11.2	16.7	4.8	5.8	6.8	8.4	5.0	2.8	*13.6*	*7.2*	—
France	17.4	9.2	15.0	6.6	21.4	3.7	7.0	9.6	15.2	6.4	2.1	5.4	*13.9*	*7.1*	—
Germany, Fed. Rep. of	19.4	6.9	16.0	10.4	13.0	4.1	5.2	10.0	7.8	6.3	3.8	3.4	*13.1*	*5.8*	—
Ireland	9.4	22.4	24.4	9.7	18.1	12.3	11.6	9.1	9.3	8.1	7.4	13.8	*16.8*	*10.2*	—
Italy	17.1	9.3	35.3	12.4	12.9	7.5	7.1	11.6	8.5	6.4	4.9	11.7	*17.4*	*8.2*	—
Netherlands	6.7	8.1	13.2	8.1	9.0	5.4	4.2	9.9	8.5	2.6	3.2	4.2	*9.0*	*5.4*	—
Average ERM[3]	**12.9**	**10.5**	**18.8**	**9.6**	**13.6**	**7.8**	**6.1**	**8.5**	**11.1**	**6.2**	**4.3**	**6.5**	*13.1*	*7.2*	n/a
Austria	10.8	5.5	9.9	7.2	6.9	6.1	4.7	8.7	5.7	5.3	5.2	4.0	*8.0*	*5.6*	0.003
Canada	14.2	25.6	19.8	10.3	32.6	18.9	19.8	30.2	30.2	14.6	29.9	26.0	*20.5*	*24.2*	0.137
Japan	19.7	19.5	16.7	15.1	30.2	20.3	29.7	28.4	16.5	12.6	22.7	24.9	*20.2*	*22.2*	0.124
Norway	6.3	9.8	7.7	12.1	13.1	7.6	11.5	16.7	22.7	8.5	9.6	9.6	*9.8*	*12.3*	0.074
Sweden	10.2	7.2	7.2	24.2	9.6	6.7	11.6	32.1	39.1	8.5	14.3	11.1	*11.7*	*17.7*	—
Switzerland	17.4	10.9	12.2	17.5	34.2	10.8	12.0	17.8	13.1	11.0	10.7	10.1	*18.4*	*12.2*	0.001
United Kingdom	11.6	9.5	22.9	10.7	15.9	29.0	13.9	28.9	22.7	25.5	13.3	26.5	*14.1*	*22.8*	—
United States	18.2	23.5	9.6	10.1	21.3	14.5	28.1	37.6	32.3	15.6	31.2	34.4	*16.5*	*27.7*	—
Average non-ERM[3]	**13.6**	**13.9**	**13.2**	**13.4**	**20.5**	**14.2**	**16.4**	**25.1**	**22.8**	**12.7**	**17.1**	**18.3**	*14.9*	*18.1*	n/a
Average European non-ERM[3]	**11.3**	**8.5**	**12.0**	**14.3**	**16.0**	**12.0**	**10.8**	**20.8**	**20.7**	**11.8**	**10.6**	**12.3**	*12.4*	*14.1*	n/a

Sources: International Monetary Fund, *International Financial Statistics,* various issues; and Fund staff calculations.

[1] Variability of weighted average (MERM weights) of bilateral real exchange rates (nominal exchange rates adjusted for relative consumer price movements—wholesale prices for Ireland) against ERM currencies, with variability measured by the standard deviation (multiplied by 1,000) of changes in the natural logarithm of the effective exchange rate index.

[2] Probability that the variance of the change in the natural logarithm of the effective exchange rate index in period 1 (January 1974 to February 1979) is equal to corresponding variance in period 2 (March 1979 to December 1985), where the effective exchange rate index is a weighted average of the given country's exchange rate with respect to the ERM currencies; MERM weights were used.

[3] Unweighted average.

Table 22.   Variability of Bilateral Nominal Exchange Rates Against Non-ERM Currencies, 1974–1985[1]

	1974	1975	1976	1977	1978	1979	1980	1981	1982	1983	1984	1985	Average 1974–78	Average 1979–85
Belgium	36.6	40.8	29.4	31.1	45.7	33.8	43.9	53.1	57.1	52.3	36.1	57.0	*36.7*	*47.6*
Denmark	32.6	33.6	25.5	30.6	39.0	30.3	38.8	53.7	45.9	47.3	34.0	55.9	*32.3*	*43.7*
France	34.1	34.5	47.8	27.0	45.9	35.6	44.4	60.7	57.6	65.1	39.7	61.8	*37.8*	*52.1*
Germany, Fed. Rep. of	34.3	35.1	30.0	32.6	46.4	39.3	45.9	48.1	33.1	38.6	36.3	53.5	*35.7*	*42.1*
Ireland	18.1	47.5	61.4	25.7	32.3	29.1	43.4	57.7	36.8	63.9	39.2	65.4	*37.0*	*47.9*
Italy	24.8	28.7	70.4	26.3	39.9	32.0	53.9	65.0	39.9	55.6	39.2	50.0	*38.0*	*47.9*
Netherlands	35.4	38.9	35.4	28.8	45.7	32.5	40.6	57.6	33.1	45.8	42.2	66.5	*36.8*	*45.5*
Average ERM[2]	**30.8**	**37.0**	**42.8**	**28.9**	**42.1**	**33.2**	**44.4**	**56.6**	**43.4**	**52.6**	**38.1**	**58.6**	*36.3*	*46.7*
Austria	44.0	38.0	33.4	35.3	46.9	49.9	45.5	51.5	35.3	43.1	40.7	62.5	*39.5*	*46.5*
Canada	12.9	16.7	17.0	34.1	36.1	18.3	18.3	17.0	24.6	7.3	23.5	26.8	*23.4*	*19.4*
Japan	33.3	22.1	22.1	59.5	96.7	68.3	64.7	48.5	54.5	18.4	33.6	84.8	*46.7*	*53.3*
Norway	30.5	40.2	30.7	34.4	42.4	29.9	30.0	42.9	61.1	22.7	42.3	51.7	*35.6*	*40.1*
Sweden	33.4	37.3	25.8	64.2	38.7	30.6	28.2	65.5	79.7	24.4	30.3	48.8	*39.9*	*43.9*
Switzerland	63.1	28.1	18.7	57.4	72.8	38.1	43.0	62.1	46.4	29.1	44.2	72.4	*48.0*	*47.9*
United Kingdom	25.7	56.4	82.5	34.4	48.8	54.0	34.4	79.9	43.7	26.4	51.1	75.7	*49.6*	*52.2*
United States	24.3	24.7	22.2	41.3	58.2	37.2	38.2	40.5	43.5	14.8	35.2	59.5	*34.2*	*38.4*
Average non-ERM[2]	**33.4**	**32.9**	**31.5**	**45.1**	**55.1**	**40.8**	**37.8**	**51.0**	**48.6**	**23.3**	**37.6**	**60.3**	*39.6*	*42.8*
Average European non-ERM[2]	**39.3**	**40.0**	**38.2**	**45.1**	**49.9**	**40.5**	**36.2**	**60.4**	**53.2**	**29.2**	**41.7**	**62.2**	*42.5*	*46.2*

Sources: International Monetary Fund, *International Financial Statistics,* various issues; and Fund staff calculations.

[1] Weighted average (MERM weights) of variability of bilateral nominal exchange rates against non-ERM currencies, with variability measured by coefficient of variation (multiplied by 1,000) of average monthly bilateral exchange rates.

[2] Unweighted average.

Table 23. Variability of Log Changes of Bilateral Nominal Exchange Rates Against Non-ERM Currencies, 1974–85[1]

	1974	1975	1976	1977	1978	1979	1980	1981	1982	1983	1984	1985	Average 1974–78	Average 1979–85
Belgium	17.2	17.5	13.2	15.0	26.6	15.7	23.0	30.8	32.4	14.2	21.9	26.2	17.9	23.4
Denmark	17.5	17.2	12.7	15.7	21.8	18.1	21.1	31.4	28.8	14.5	19.5	25.4	17.0	22.7
France	18.2	23.2	15.8	11.7	24.5	15.6	22.8	31.4	31.1	15.1	22.8	26.9	18.7	23.7
Germany, Fed. Rep. of	19.3	17.3	12.7	15.3	25.6	15.0	21.4	31.9	23.5	14.8	21.7	25.3	18.0	21.9
Ireland	10.9	12.1	21.2	9.4	18.3	16.2	23.2	31.3	23.7	17.4	21.8	28.4	14.4	23.1
Italy	16.8	14.0	39.1	10.0	20.8	14.4	22.2	27.1	24.5	11.6	20.0	25.5	20.1	20.8
Netherlands	16.8	19.2	14.9	14.5	26.7	16.2	22.8	35.2	24.1	14.7	23.7	28.1	18.4	23.6
Average ERM[2]	**16.7**	**17.2**	**18.5**	**13.1**	**23.5**	**15.9**	**22.4**	**31.3**	**26.9**	**14.6**	**21.6**	**26.5**	*17.8*	*22.7*
Austria	19.0	18.5	13.1	15.8	26.5	18.1	24.1	35.0	25.5	16.0	24.5	27.9	18.6	24.4
Canada	8.6	9.7	14.4	12.9	16.4	14.1	13.2	10.8	17.8	5.4	11.5	14.6	12.4	12.5
Japan	20.0	12.8	11.3	18.5	37.7	23.3	36.9	21.6	40.1	16.9	19.4	31.7	20.1	27.1
Norway	15.8	21.9	13.5	17.8	24.8	13.3	18.1	20.7	26.6	13.1	18.4	22.9	18.7	19.0
Sweden	16.5	18.9	12.3	26.9	18.3	12.1	17.6	17.7	42.7	10.0	16.7	20.3	18.6	19.6
Switzerland	24.7	19.5	9.9	21.8	41.9	16.3	28.5	40.8	28.3	12.8	19.7	33.3	23.6	25.7
United Kingdom	14.3	14.8	26.6	13.6	25.1	25.2	21.3	24.6	25.7	19.6	19.7	34.7	18.9	24.4
United States	15.3	12.3	12.6	15.1	25.0	18.2	24.6	18.6	27.8	11.8	17.1	25.3	16.0	20.5
Average non-ERM[2]	**16.8**	**16.0**	**14.2**	**17.8**	**26.9**	**17.6**	**23.1**	**23.7**	**29.3**	**13.2**	**18.4**	**26.3**	*18.4*	*21.7*
Average European non-ERM[2]	**18.1**	**18.7**	**15.1**	**19.2**	**27.3**	**17.0**	**21.9**	**27.8**	**29.7**	**14.3**	**19.8**	**27.8**	*19.7*	*22.6*

Sources: International Monetary Fund, *International Financial Statistics*, various issues; and Fund staff calculations.

[1] Weighted average (MERM weights) of variability of bilateral nominal exchange rates against non-ERM currencies, with variability measured by the standard deviation (multiplied by 1,000) of changes in the natural logarithm of average monthly bilateral exchange rates.

[2] Unweighted average.

Table 24.   Variability of Log Changes of Nominal Effective Exchange Rates Against Non-ERM Currencies, 1974–85[1]

	1974	1975	1976	1977	1978	1979	1980	1981	1982	1983	1984	1985	Average 1974–78	Average 1979–85	F probabilities[2]
Belgium	13.6	15.3	11.5	10.2	20.0	11.2	17.3	27.2	26.0	11.4	20.1	21.6	14.1	19.2	0.008
Denmark	15.0	14.7	9.7	10.0	15.7	14.4	16.5	28.7	21.3	11.9	17.3	21.0	13.0	18.7	0.003
France	14.7	21.7	13.1	5.4	15.9	10.4	16.4	27.8	25.1	12.4	21.2	21.8	14.1	19.3	0.007
Germany, Fed. Rep. of	16.4	15.3	10.0	10.5	18.5	9.8	15.1	28.9	13.9	12.4	20.2	20.2	14.2	17.2	0.029
Ireland	8.2	10.3	20.8	6.3	14.1	9.9	19.5	28.3	17.6	15.1	19.9	27.9	11.9	19.0	0.005
Italy	12.6	10.2	37.7	5.8	9.8	7.2	15.3	22.2	15.2	7.1	17.2	18.3	15.2	14.6	0.301
Netherlands	13.7	17.4	12.6	10.0	20.9	11.4	17.6	33.0	15.2	12.2	22.3	23.9	14.9	19.4	0.010
Average ERM[3]	**13.5**	**15.0**	**16.5**	**8.3**	**16.4**	**10.6**	**16.8**	**28.0**	**19.2**	**11.8**	**19.7**	**21.4**	*13.9*	*18.2*	n/a
Austria	16.1	16.4	10.5	10.6	19.3	13.9	18.2	32.4	15.5	13.7	23.1	23.1	14.6	20.0	0.006
Canada	5.1	8.3	13.9	11.8	14.8	12.4	8.1	6.4	14.2	3.5	9.2	9.2	10.8	9.0	0.116
Japan	18.7	10.2	9.2	17.0	36.4	22.0	36.0	18.7	38.7	15.8	17.1	29.0	18.3	25.3	0.017
Norway	12.4	20.9	10.8	13.4	18.3	6.4	11.0	15.8	16.5	9.2	15.8	15.3	15.2	12.8	0.244
Sweden	13.4	16.8	9.9	25.2	5.2	4.7	9.8	11.1	38.7	4.1	12.3	12.0	14.1	13.2	0.541
Switzerland	22.5	17.3	8.0	18.9	38.2	12.2	23.5	39.2	20.3	10.4	17.2	30.9	21.0	22.0	0.615
United Kingdom	8.3	11.0	25.9	8.2	17.1	22.7	13.4	20.2	17.7	17.7	16.8	30.7	14.1	19.9	0.031
United States	13.6	8.7	6.4	8.9	16.8	13.0	22.1	16.5	21.8	9.8	14.0	22.0	10.9	17.0	—
Average non-ERM[3]	**13.8**	**13.7**	**11.8**	**14.3**	**20.8**	**13.4**	**17.7**	**20.0**	**22.9**	**10.5**	**15.7**	**21.5**	*14.9*	*17.4*	n/a
Average European non-ERM[3]	**14.6**	**16.5**	**13.0**	**15.3**	**19.6**	**12.0**	**15.2**	**23.7**	**21.7**	**11.0**	**17.0**	**22.4**	*15.8*	*17.6*	n/a

Sources: International Monetary Fund, *International Financial Statistics,* various issues; and Fund staff calculations.

[1] Variability of weighted average (MERM weights) of bilateral nominal exchange rates against non-ERM currencies, with variability measured by the standard deviation (multiplied by 1,000) of changes in the natural logarithm of the effective exchange rate index.

[2] Probability that the variance of the change in the natural logarithm of the effective exchange rate index in period 1 (January 1974 to February 1979) is equal to corresponding variance in period 2 (March 1979 to December 1985), where the effective exchange rate index is a weighted average of the given country's exchange rate with respect to the ERM currencies; MERM weights were used.

[3] Unweighted average.

Table 25. Variability of Bilateral Real Exchange Rates Against Non-ERM Currencies, 1974–85[1]

	1974	1975	1976	1977	1978	1979	1980	1981	1982	1983	1984	1985	Average 1974–78	Average 1979–85
Belgium	42.8	35.7	31.0	27.9	40.8	36.6	50.6	56.4	50.5	44.6	36.0	55.9	35.6	47.2
Denmark	38.7	41.5	38.7	28.9	38.3	35.2	40.9	50.0	41.9	44.2	32.7	54.4	37.2	42.7
France	34.7	31.1	38.5	27.2	44.8	41.3	41.7	52.6	51.7	51.0	36.2	64.2	35.3	48.4
Germany, Fed. Rep. of	29.1	43.4	24.3	27.8	38.7	35.8	58.9	50.1	33.8	42.2	40.5	49.9	32.7	44.5
Ireland	25.3	49.3	36.7	25.6	29.6	29.6	44.5	52.4	37.1	52.6	38.7	65.8	33.3	45.8
Italy	26.4	23.9	49.2	26.4	36.0	48.6	38.1	51.1	34.6	36.5	34.1	50.4	32.4	41.9
Netherlands	30.6	36.6	38.4	25.4	39.8	35.1	48.9	61.4	34.6	48.3	44.9	63.1	34.2	48.0
Average ERM[2]	**32.5**	**37.3**	**36.7**	**27.0**	**38.3**	**37.5**	**46.2**	**53.4**	**40.6**	**45.6**	**37.6**	**57.7**	*34.4*	*45.5*
Austria	34.9	42.5	30.4	29.6	39.2	43.3	56.4	55.2	36.9	46.0	42.8	59.3	35.3	48.6
Canada	14.0	14.8	17.2	26.5	36.4	22.8	18.3	22.1	25.3	8.4	25.1	26.4	21.8	21.2
Japan	30.6	21.4	28.1	52.6	84.9	84.6	57.0	59.7	59.6	21.9	37.6	82.0	43.5	57.5
Norway	23.2	36.5	28.5	30.3	39.3	35.9	29.8	43.2	53.1	20.4	40.7	54.2	31.6	39.6
Sweden	28.6	32.7	28.8	48.0	32.1	33.2	29.8	66.8	73.7	18.7	29.1	49.6	34.0	43.0
Switzerland	53.6	36.4	14.8	50.1	61.1	33.8	52.8	62.7	42.8	33.2	48.2	67.2	43.2	48.7
United Kingdom	30.0	30.4	62.6	33.3	43.0	77.2	36.8	69.8	42.6	25.5	47.6	81.9	39.9	54.5
United States	24.9	21.1	23.6	35.9	51.8	46.5	36.7	47.1	44.7	16.6	37.6	58.6	31.4	41.1
Average non-ERM[2]	**30.0**	**29.5**	**29.2**	**38.3**	**48.5**	**47.2**	**39.7**	**53.3**	**47.3**	**23.9**	**38.6**	**59.9**	*35.1*	*44.3*
Average European non-ERM[2]	**34.1**	**35.7**	**33.0**	**38.3**	**42.9**	**44.7**	**41.1**	**59.5**	**49.8**	**28.8**	**41.7**	**62.5**	*36.8*	*46.9*

Sources: International Monetary Fund, *International Financial Statistics,* various issues; and Fund staff calculations.

[1] Weighted average (MERM weights) of variability of bilateral real exchange rates (nominal exchange rates adjusted for relative consumer price movements—wholesale prices for Ireland) against non-ERM currencies, with variability measured by the coefficient of variation (multiplied by 1,000) of average monthly bilateral exchange rates.

[2] Unweighted average.

Table 26. Variability of Log Changes of Bilateral Real Exchange Rates Against Non-ERM Currencies, 1974–85[1]

	1974	1975	1976	1977	1978	1979	1980	1981	1982	1983	1984	1985	Average 1974–78	Average 1979–85
Belgium	18.4	18.3	14.2	15.6	27.4	17.5	24.5	31.9	33.4	14.7	23.7	26.3	18.8	24.6
Denmark	18.2	20.4	19.5	19.0	24.8	22.3	23.9	31.4	28.9	15.4	21.9	25.0	20.4	24.1
France	19.4	23.1	15.6	12.2	25.1	16.7	24.6	32.1	32.4	16.0	24.5	27.9	19.1	24.9
Germany, Fed. Rep. of	21.2	19.0	14.2	16.1	26.2	16.2	23.1	32.4	23.8	14.7	23.8	25.7	19.3	22.8
Ireland	20.1	25.0	21.0	10.4	18.5	18.8	20.1	29.3	22.9	17.0	22.3	31.9	19.0	23.2
Italy	20.5	15.6	35.1	10.4	21.3	16.4	23.7	26.7	25.0	14.6	22.1	26.2	20.6	22.1
Netherlands	18.1	20.3	18.7	14.9	27.7	17.7	24.6	37.3	24.6	15.7	25.8	28.4	20.0	24.8
Average ERM[2]	**19.4**	**20.3**	**19.7**	**14.1**	**24.4**	**18.0**	**23.5**	**31.6**	**27.3**	**15.4**	**23.4**	**27.3**	*19.6*	*23.8*
Austria	21.4	19.4	15.0	17.0	27.3	20.1	26.6	35.9	25.9	17.3	28.1	28.7	20.0	26.1
Canada	10.2	10.2	14.9	12.4	20.0	15.4	14.5	11.8	18.6	8.9	11.7	15.3	13.5	13.7
Japan	25.3	14.9	16.3	17.4	39.1	24.3	39.1	24.3	41.5	21.8	20.1	34.9	22.6	29.4
Norway	17.8	22.2	12.2	18.8	24.9	15.1	20.4	21.9	27.8	14.4	20.6	23.6	19.2	20.5
Sweden	18.7	20.5	14.6	27.8	19.0	13.7	21.2	18.5	40.3	11.7	18.2	20.8	20.1	20.6
Switzerland	26.7	21.6	10.7	24.0	41.0	17.9	30.1	38.7	28.0	13.2	23.5	32.2	24.8	26.2
United Kingdom	20.2	18.8	27.1	14.3	24.8	32.9	24.2	28.2	25.2	21.6	22.2	38.4	21.1	27.5
United States	18.8	13.7	14.7	14.5	26.8	19.7	26.3	20.5	28.9	15.1	17.5	27.0	17.7	27.1
Average non-ERM[2]	**19.9**	**17.7**	**15.7**	**18.3**	**27.9**	**19.9**	**25.3**	**25.0**	**29.5**	**15.5**	**20.2**	**27.6**	*19.9*	*23.3*
Average European non-ERM[2]	**21.0**	**20.5**	**15.9**	**20.4**	**27.4**	**19.9**	**24.5**	**28.7**	**29.4**	**15.6**	**22.5**	**28.7**	*21.0*	*24.2*

Sources: International Monetary Fund, *International Financial Statistics,* various issues; and Fund staff calculations.

[1] Weighted average (MERM weights) of variability of bilateral real exchange rates (nominal exchange rates adjusted for relative consumer price movements—wholesale prices for Ireland) against non-ERM currencies, with variability measured by the standard deviation (multiplied by 1,000) of changes in the natural logarithm of average monthly bilateral exchange rates.

[2] Unweighted average.

Table 27. Variability of Real Effective Exchange Rates Against Non-ERM Currencies, 1974–85[1]

	1974	1975	1976	1977	1978	1979	1980	1981	1982	1983	1984	1985	Average 1974–78	Average 1979–85	F probabilities[2]
Belgium	13.0	15.5	11.1	10.9	20.8	12.6	18.0	28.2	26.9	10.7	21.1	20.4	14.2	19.7	0.008
Denmark	14.0	17.2	16.7	14.1	19.3	17.9	18.7	28.3	21.4	11.7	19.3	18.9	16.3	19.5	0.130
France	14.5	21.3	11.8	6.1	16.2	10.5	17.6	28.2	27.0	12.0	22.1	21.9	14.0	19.9	0.004
Germany, Fed. Rep. of	17.3	16.5	10.5	11.2	19.2	9.9	15.4	28.9	14.2	10.6	21.5	19.4	14.9	17.1	0.079
Ireland	16.6	22.8	18.5	6.3	13.0	10.9	13.8	25.1	16.3	13.8	19.6	25.2	15.5	17.8	0.836
Italy	15.6	11.4	33.4	6.0	10.4	9.3	15.9	21.4	15.7	9.7	18.8	17.8	15.3	15.5	0.854
Netherlands	13.4	17.9	16.1	10.6	21.7	12.2	18.7	35.0	15.8	12.3	23.8	23.1	15.9	20.1	0.015
Average ERM[3]	**14.9**	**17.5**	**16.9**	**9.3**	**17.2**	**11.9**	**16.9**	**27.9**	**19.6**	**11.5**	**20.9**	**21.0**	*15.2*	*18.5*	n/a
Austria	17.3	16.7	11.6	12.2	19.8	15.4	20.1	33.1	16.3	13.8	26.3	22.9	15.5	21.1	0.009
Canada	6.1	8.9	14.1	11.0	18.4	13.4	9.1	6.9	14.5	7.3	9.3	9.7	11.7	10.0	0.136
Japan	23.9	12.2	14.9	15.8	37.9	22.3	38.0	21.3	40.2	21.0	17.5	32.4	20.9	27.5	0.019
Norway	12.3	20.1	7.4	14.8	18.0	7.3	12.1	16.0	18.5	9.2	17.3	14.0	14.5	13.5	0.208
Sweden	14.0	17.7	12.1	26.2	7.4	6.6	13.4	11.4	35.7	4.5	13.1	10.5	15.5	13.6	0.578
Switzerland	23.6	19.4	8.3	21.5	36.9	13.8	24.4	36.6	19.7	8.3	20.8	28.9	21.9	21.8	0.838
United Kingdom	15.2	15.5	26.0	9.5	16.7	30.9	16.3	24.2	16.2	19.1	19.0	34.4	16.6	22.8	0.006
United States	16.4	9.1	7.8	8.4	17.2	14.0	23.3	18.4	23.6	11.3	13.8	13.2	11.8	18.2	—
Average non-ERM[3]	**16.1**	**15.0**	**12.8**	**14.9**	**21.5**	**15.4**	**19.6**	**21.0**	**23.1**	**11.8**	**17.1**	**22.0**	*16.1*	*18.6*	n/a
Average European non-ERM[3]	**16.5**	**17.9**	**13.1**	**16.8**	**19.8**	**14.8**	**17.2**	**24.3**	**21.3**	**11.0**	**19.3**	**22.1**	*16.8*	*18.6*	n/a

Sources: International Monetary Fund, *International Financial Statistics,* various issues; and Fund staff calculations.

[1] Variability of weighted average (MERM weights) of bilateral real exchange rates (nominal exchange rates adjusted for relative consumer price movements—wholesale prices for Ireland) against non-ERM currencies, with variability measured by the standard deviation (multiplied by 1,000) of changes in the natural logarithm of the effective exchange rate index.

[2] Probability that the variance of the change in the natural logarithm of the effective exchange rate index in period 1 (January 1974 to February 1979) is equal to corresponding variance in period 2 (March 1979 to December 1985), where the effective exchange rate index is a weighted average of the given country's exchange rate with respect to the ERM currencies; MERM weights were used.

[3] Unweighted average.

Table 28. Variability of Nominal Effective Exchange Rates, 1974–85[1]

	1974	1975	1976	1977	1978	1979	1980	1981	1982	1983	1984	1985	Average 1974–78	Average 1979–85
Belgium	18.6	23.2	27.6	9.4	15.4	9.3	14.5	14.5	35.9	20.2	8.3	18.6	18.8	17.3
Denmark	21.0	18.5	24.8	18.0	14.4	17.3	20.1	24.4	19.5	27.6	14.0	32.1	19.3	22.1
France	26.3	21.9	40.3	5.4	17.0	14.9	18.3	31.5	40.8	40.4	17.4	34.6	22.2	28.3
Germany, Fed. Rep. of	25.7	23.6	36.5	20.2	20.4	23.0	23.9	22.4	15.9	15.2	18.6	30.2	25.3	21.3
Ireland	10.8	39.6	63.1	16.3	19.9	12.4	22.9	23.3	10.7	39.4	17.0	33.4	29.9	22.7
Italy	31.6	5.4	63.4	14.7	20.2	8.6	28.9	39.5	15.7	28.9	17.7	15.7	27.1	22.1
Netherlands	15.9	19.5	33.5	8.1	16.8	11.0	13.1	26.0	14.7	14.6	16.9	33.2	18.8	18.5
Average ERM[2]	**21.4**	**21.7**	**41.3**	**13.1**	**17.7**	**13.8**	**20.2**	**25.9**	**21.9**	**26.6**	**15.7**	**28.3**	*23.1*	*21.8*
Austria	31.4	21.4	31.8	17.2	14.2	32.9	22.4	23.9	10.0	20.5	20.6	35.6	23.2	23.7
Canada	6.8	15.1	16.2	33.2	39.5	14.3	7.2	17.3	19.8	11.1	14.6	33.3	22.2	16.8
Japan	31.5	10.0	21.7	53.6	85.5	71.0	70.3	21.4	35.1	24.2	11.4	56.4	40.4	41.4
Norway	15.3	25.6	26.6	21.5	23.1	8.8	7.4	10.3	44.1	8.6	25.8	17.6	22.4	17.5
Sweden	24.4	22.8	21.2	60.7	1.9	14.6	4.3	49.6	67.1	4.3	5.3	11.8	26.2	22.4
Switzerland	54.7	13.0	24.8	54.0	59.4	18.4	18.5	55.9	24.1	6.9	25.8	48.3	41.2	28.3
United Kingdom	12.2	41.8	71.6	12.7	26.2	40.2	30.1	58.3	20.0	23.5	33.2	51.0	32.9	36.6
United States	18.7	29.9	7.5	14.3	35.7	10.3	23.6	48.8	44.3	30.4	43.6	61.1	21.2	37.4
Average non-ERM[2]	**24.4**	**22.5**	**27.7**	**33.4**	**35.7**	**26.3**	**23.0**	**35.7**	**33.1**	**16.2**	**22.5**	**39.4**	*28.7*	*28.0*
Average European non-ERM[2]	**27.6**	**24.9**	**35.2**	**33.2**	**25.0**	**23.0**	**16.5**	**39.6**	**33.1**	**12.7**	**22.1**	**32.9**	*29.2*	*25.7*

Sources: International Monetary Fund, *International Financial Statistics,* various issues; and Fund staff calculations.

[1] Based on the IMF's multilateral exchange rate model (MERM) and monthly data. Variability is measured by the coefficient of variation (multiplied by 1,000) of average monthly effective exchange rates.

[2] Unweighted average.

Table 29. Variability of Log Changes of Nominal Effective Exchange Rates, 1974–85[1]

	1974	1975	1976	1977	1978	1979	1980	1981	1982	1983	1984	1985	Average 1974–78	Average 1979–85	F probabilities[2]
Belgium	10.6	8.0	9.2	7.3	12.5	6.4	7.4	9.7	19.5	6.2	7.2	7.7	*9.5*	*9.2*	0.877
Denmark	11.6	10.2	10.2	9.4	11.9	14.1	10.3	18.0	14.1	9.5	9.6	12.7	*10.7*	*12.6*	0.229
France	18.6	14.8	12.8	4.9	15.2	6.8	8.6	15.0	17.3	9.6	10.7	11.4	*13.3*	*11.4*	0.538
Germany, Fed. Rep. of	18.6	11.3	11.4	9.8	14.8	6.8	8.9	18.9	7.6	9.4	12.0	12.0	*13.2*	*10.8*	0.306
Ireland	7.5	8.3	22.8	8.2	15.9	7.2	11.8	15.5	8.8	10.6	11.6	12.3	*12.5*	*11.1*	0.142
Italy	19.5	4.3	36.5	7.8	7.9	5.7	8.2	10.0	7.9	5.2	7.2	9.9	*15.2*	*7.7*	—
Netherlands	8.9	15.2	9.4	7.6	13.2	7.4	7.8	17.6	5.8	6.5	9.5	10.9	*10.9*	*9.4*	0.250
Average ERM[3]	**13.6**	**10.3**	**16.0**	**7.9**	**13.1**	**7.8**	**9.0**	**15.0**	**11.6**	**8.2**	**9.7**	**11.0**	***12.2***	***10.3***	n/a
Austria	13.4	13.8	8.2	8.7	12.7	9.9	10.9	20.1	8.3	9.6	13.2	13.3	*11.4*	*12.2*	0.264
Canada	5.1	11.0	13.3	11.9	16.8	12.9	6.5	4.8	14.5	4.4	11.3	8.7	*11.6*	*9.0*	0.106
Japan	17.1	9.6	9.7	15.1	31.9	19.6	29.6	20.7	29.7	14.3	12.1	23.3	*16.7*	*21.3*	0.066
Norway	9.9	14.9	9.0	11.9	14.8	4.5	7.3	9.2	14.8	8.2	9.2	7.5	*12.1*	*8.7*	0.022
Sweden	12.3	14.9	7.4	23.3	2.7	2.9	4.1	15.9	35.0	3.3	5.7	4.9	*12.1*	*10.3*	0.763
Switzerland	20.6	12.8	9.3	18.5	35.0	9.7	16.5	28.3	16.0	12.7	9.1	22.0	*19.3*	*16.3*	0.185
United Kingdom	8.1	8.8	24.1	9.4	17.6	20.8	10.5	21.8	17.5	22.6	9.5	26.8	*13.6*	*18.5*	0.037
United States	13.3	16.4	5.2	8.3	15.9	11.2	21.8	21.9	23.2	12.9	19.4	27.0	*11.8*	*19.6*	—
Average non-ERM[3]	**12.5**	**12.8**	**10.8**	**13.4**	**18.4**	**11.4**	**13.4**	**17.8**	**19.9**	**11.0**	**11.2**	**16.7**	***13.6***	***14.5***	n/a
Average European non-ERM[3]	**12.9**	**13.1**	**11.6**	**14.4**	**16.6**	**9.6**	**9.9**	**19.1**	**18.3**	**11.3**	**9.3**	**14.9**	***13.7***	***13.2***	n/a

Sources: International Monetary Fund, *International Financial Statistics,* various issues; and Fund staff calculations.

[1] Based on the Fund's multilateral exchange rate model (MERM) and monthly data. Variability is measured by the standard deviation (multiplied by 1,000) of the change in the natural logarithm of the average monthly exchange rates.

[2] Probability that the variance of the change in the natural logarithm of the effective exchange rate index in period 1 (January 1974 to February 1979) is equal to corresponding variance in period 2 (March 1979 to December 1985).

[3] Unweighted average.

Table 30.   Variability of Nominal Exchange Rates Against ERM Currencies, 1979–1985[1]

	1979	1980	1981	1982	1983	1984	1985	Average 1979–85
Belgium	8.2	6.5	16.9	35.6	12.4	6.5	9.2	13.6
Denmark	25.0	8.2	17.5	19.4	12.1	7.5	13.2	14.7
France	9.3	7.6	21.6	35.1	19.9	3.8	14.1	15.9
Germany, Fed. Rep. of	12.2	6.9	27.2	31.2	18.3	4.1	12.6	16.1
Ireland	12.0	7.4	15.5	20.4	14.5	5.8	9.9	12.2
Italy	14.3	11.9	27.5	23.8	14.6	6.3	35.9	19.2
Netherlands	9.3	7.4	22.4	25.6	11.9	3.5	10.8	13.0
Average ERM[2]	**12.9**	**8.0**	**21.2**	**27.3**	**14.8**	**5.3**	**15.1**	**15.0**
Austria	16.3	6.4	20.1	18.4	10.9	3.4	8.7	12.0
Canada	27.7	30.7	65.1	47.6	54.5	45.4	86.7	51.1
Japan	76.0	85.2	35.1	28.5	54.4	28.2	27.5	47.8
Norway	12.6	24.3	26.7	40.5	33.7	10.6	19.7	24.0
Sweden	13.9	22.1	49.8	66.8	29.2	16.9	21.5	31.5
Switzerland	11.8	17.6	63.5	24.8	29.0	14.5	21.4	26.1
United Kingdom	36.1	51.6	45.1	30.2	44.2	19.9	38.7	38.0
United States	23.4	41.3	69.7	51.6	57.3	57.4	83.5	54.9
Average non-ERM[2]	**27.2**	**34.9**	**46.9**	**38.6**	**39.1**	**24.5**	**38.4**	**35.7**
Average European non-ERM[2]	**18.1**	**24.4**	**41.1**	**36.2**	**29.4**	**13.1**	**22.0**	**26.3**

Sources: International Monetary Fund, *International Financial Statistics,* various issues; and Fund staff calculations.

[1] Weighted average (MERM weights) of variability of bilateral nominal exchange rate against ERM currencies, with variability measured by coefficient of variation (multiplied by 1,000) of daily bilateral exchange rates. Based on daily data.

[2] Unweighted average.

Table 31. Consumer Price Indices, 1974–85

(Annual change in percent)

	1974	1975	1976	1977	1978	Average 1974–78	1979	1980	1981	1982	1983	1984	1985	Average 1979–85
Belgium	12.7	12.8	9.2	7.1	4.5	9.2	4.5	6.6	7.6	8.7	7.7	6.3	4.9	6.6
Denmark	15.2	9.6	9.0	11.1	10.1	11.0	9.6	12.3	11.7	10.1	6.9	6.3	4.7	8.8
France	13.7	11.8	9.6	9.4	9.1	10.7	10.7	13.8	13.4	11.8	9.6	7.4	5.8	10.3
Germany	7.0	5.9	4.3	3.7	2.7	4.7	4.1	5.4	6.3	5.3	3.3	2.4	2.2	4.1
Ireland	17.0	20.9	18.0	13.6	7.6	15.3	13.2	18.2	20.4	17.1	10.5	8.6	5.4	13.2
Italy	19.1	17.0	16.8	17.0	12.1	16.4	14.8	21.2	17.8	16.5	14.7	10.8	9.2	14.9
Netherlands	9.6	10.5	9.0	6.5	4.2	7.9	4.2	6.5	6.7	5.9	2.8	3.3	2.2	4.5
Arithmetic average ERM	**13.5**	**12.6**	**10.8**	**9.8**	**7.2**	*10.7*	**8.7**	**12.0**	**12.0**	**10.8**	**7.9**	**6.4**	**4.9**	*8.9*
Standard deviation	3.9	4.6	4.5	4.2	3.2	3.8	4.2	5.7	5.2	4.3	3.9	2.7	2.2	3.9
Difference between highest and lowest value	12.2	14.9	13.7	13.3	9.5	11.7	10.7	15.8	14.1	11.8	11.9	8.4	7.0	10.8
Coefficient of variation	0.29	0.36	0.41	0.43	0.45	0.35	0.48	0.48	0.43	0.40	0.49	0.42	0.45	0.43
Weighted average	**11.7**	**10.4**	**8.7**	**8.1**	**6.5**	...	**8.0**	**11.1**	**10.9**	**9.7**	**7.6**	**5.9**	**4.9**	...
Australia	15.1	15.1	13.5	12.3	7.9	12.8	9.1	10.1	9.7	11.1	10.1	4.0	6.7	8.7
Austria	9.5	8.4	7.3	5.5	3.6	6.9	3.7	6.4	6.8	5.4	3.3	5.7	3.2	4.9
Canada	10.9	10.8	7.5	8.0	9.0	9.2	9.1	10.2	12.4	10.8	5.8	4.3	4.0	8.1
Finland	16.7	17.8	14.4	12.7	7.8	13.8	7.5	11.6	12.0	9.3	8.4	7.1	5.9	8.8
Greece	26.9	13.4	13.3	12.1	12.6	15.5	19.0	24.9	24.5	21.0	20.2	18.4	19.3	21.0
Iceland	43.0	49.0	32.2	30.5	44.1	39.5	45.5	58.5	50.6	49.1	86.1	30.8	32.0	49.4
Japan	24.4	11.8	9.3	8.0	3.8	11.3	3.6	8.0	4.9	2.6	1.8	2.3	2.0	3.6
New Zealand	11.2	14.5	17.1	14.4	11.9	13.8	13.6	17.2	15.3	16.2	7.3	6.2	15.4	13.0
Norway	9.4	11.6	9.2	9.1	8.0	9.5	4.8	10.8	13.7	11.4	8.4	6.3	5.7	8.7
Portugal	28.0	20.4	18.2	27.1	22.7	23.2	23.6	16.6	20.0	22.7	25.1	28.9	19.6	22.3
Spain	15.7	17.0	15.0	24.5	19.8	18.3	15.7	15.6	14.6	14.4	12.2	11.3	8.8	13.2
Sweden	9.9	9.8	10.3	11.5	9.9	10.3	7.2	13.7	12.1	8.6	8.9	8.0	7.4	9.4
Switzerland	9.8	6.7	1.7	1.3	1.1	4.1	3.6	4.0	6.5	5.7	3.0	2.9	3.4	4.1
United Kingdom	15.9	24.3	16.6	15.8	8.3	16.1	13.4	18.0	11.9	8.6	4.6	5.0	6.1	9.6
United States	11.0	9.1	5.8	6.5	7.6	8.0	11.3	13.5	10.4	6.2	3.2	4.3	3.6	7.4
Arithmetic average non-ERM	**17.2**	**16.0**	**12.8**	**13.3**	**11.9**	*14.1*	**12.7**	**15.9**	**15.0**	**13.5**	**13.9**	**9.7**	**7.9**	*12.8*
Standard deviation	9.2	9.9	6.9	8.0	10.2	8.2	10.4	12.4	10.7	11.0	20.3	8.8	8.4	11.1
Coefficient of variation	0.54	0.62	0.54	0.60	0.86	0.58	0.82	0.78	0.71	0.81	1.46	0.91	1.06	0.87
Of which:														
Central European and Scandinavian Countries[1]														
Average	11.0	10.9	8.6	8,0	6.1	8.9	5.4	9.3	10.2	8.1	6.4	6.0	5.1	7.2
Standard deviation	2.8	3.8	4.1	4.2	3.2	3.3	1.7	3.6	3.0	2.3	2.7	1.7	1.6	2.2
Coefficient of variation	0.25	0.35	0.48	0.52	0.54	0.37	0.32	0.38	0.29	0.28	0.42	0.29	0.31	0.31
Southern European Countries[2]														
Average	23.5	16.9	15.5	21.3	18.3	19.0	19.4	19.0	19.7	19.4	19.2	19.5	5.9	18.8
Standard deviation	5.6	2.9	2.1	6.5	4.3	3.2	3.3	4.2	4.1	3.6	5.3	7.2	5.0	4.0
Coefficient of variation	0.24	0.17	0.13	0.31	0.23	0.17	0.17	0.22	0.21	0.18	0.28	0.37	0.32	0.21
Atlantic Countries[3]														
Average	12.6	14.7	9.9	10.1	8.3	11.1	11.3	13.9	11.6	8.5	4.5	4.5	4.6	8.3
Standard deviation	2.4	6.8	4.7	4.1	0.6	3.6	1.8	3.2	0.9	1.9	1.1	0.3	1.1	0.9
Coefficient of variation	0.19	0.46	0.48	0.40	0.07	0.32	0.16	0.23	0.08	0.22	10.23	0.07	0.24	0.11
Pacific Countries[4]														
Average	16.9	13.8	13.3	11.6	7.9	12.6	8.8	11.8	10.0	10.0	6.4	4.1	8.0	8.4
Standard deviation	5.6	1.4	3.2	2.6	3.3	1.0	4.1	3.9	4.3	5.6	3.4	1.6	5.6	3.8
Coefficient of variation	0.33	0.10	0.24	0.23	0.42	0.08	0.47	0.33	0.43	0.56	0.54	0.39	0.69	0.46

Source: International Monetary Fund, *International Financial Statistics,* various issues.
[1] Austria, Finland, Norway, Sweden, Switzerland.
[2] Greece, Portugal, Spain.
[3] Canada, United Kingdom, United States.
[4] Australia, Japan, New Zealand.

Table 32. GDP Deflators, 1974–85

(Annual change in percent)

	1974	1975	1976	1977	1978	Average 1974–78	1979	1980	1981	1982	1983	1984	Average 1979–84	1985
Belgium	12.6	12.2	7.7	7.4	4.3	8.8	4.6	3.9	5.4	7.1	5.9	5.5	5.4	5.3
Denmark	13.1	12.4	9.1	9.4	9.9	10.8	7.6	8.2	10.1	10.6	8.2	5.6	8.4	5.1
France	11.1	13.4	9.9	9.0	9.5	10.6	10.4	12.2	11.8	12.6	9.5	7.1	10.6	5.9
Germany	7.1	6.0	3.6	3.7	4.3	4.9	4.0	4.8	4.0	4.4	3.3	1.9	3.7	2.2
Ireland	6.3	22.6	21.0	13.3	10.5	14.6	13.7	14.7	18.2	15.9	10.4	6.6	13.2	6.3
Italy	18.5	17.5	18.0	19.1	13.9	17.4	15.9	20.6	18.7	17.2	15.2	10.7	16.3	8.8
Netherlands	9.1	10.2	8.9	6.7	5.5	8.1	3.8	5.5	5.4	6.3	1.6	2.6	4.2	2.5
Arithmetic average ERM	**11.1**	**13.5**	**11.2**	**9.8**	**8.3**	**10.7**	**8.6**	**10.0**	**10.5**	**10.6**	**7.7**	**5.7**	**8.8**	**5.2**
Standard deviation	3.9	4.9	5.7	4.7	3.4	3.8	4.5	5.7	5.6	4.5	4.3	2.7	4.4	2.1
Difference between highest and lowest value	12.2	16.6	17.4	15.4	9.6	12.5	12.1	16.7	14.7	12.8	13.6	8.8	12.6	6.6
Coefficient of variation	0.35	0.36	0.51	0.48	0.41	0.36	0.53	0.57	0.54	0.43	0.55	0.48	0.50	0.41
Weighted average	**10.8**	**11.0**	**8.6**	**8.3**	**7.6**	**. . .**	**7.9**	**9.4**	**9.4**	**9.9**	**7.6**	**5.6**	**. . .**	**4.9**
Australia	16.7	15.9	14.0	9.0	8.0	12.7	8.2	11.8	9.6	11.7	8.4	6.8	9.4	6.4
Austria	9.5	6.5	5.6	5.3	5.3	6.4	4.1	5.1	6.3	6.4	4.0	4.8	5.1	3.3
Canada	15.3	10.8	9.6	7.4	6.7	9.9	10.3	11.4	10.6	10.3	5.5	3.0	8.5	. . .
Finland	22.5	14.5	12.6	10.2	7.7	13.4	8.2	9.2	11.4	9.1	9.0	7.6	9.1	. . .
Greece	20.9	12.3	15.4	12.9	13.0	14.9	18.6	17.7	20.0	24.9	19.1	20.1	20.0	17.2
Iceland	41.0	39.7	34.1	35.3	46.3	39.2	40.3	52.8	50.4	54.4	79.8	26.3	49.8	. . .
Japan	20.6	7.8	6.4	5.7	4.6	8.9	2.6	2.8	2.7	1.7	0.5	0.5	1.8	. . .
New Zealand	5.7	11.6	18.4	15.8	13.5	12.9	17.3	15.1	14.9	10.6	6.2	. . .	. . .	. . .
Norway	10.3	10.0	7.5	8.3	6.4	8.5	6.6	14.5	14.0	10.2	6.2	6.6	9.6	5.5
Portugal	18.9	16.2	16.3	26.4	22.3	20.0	20.7	17.9	13.4	21.5	. . .	. . .	. . .	. . .
Spain	16.6	16.7	16.7	22.8	20.2	18.6	16.7	13.9	13.7	13.5	11.9	11.3	13.5	. . .
Sweden	9.5	14.5	11.9	10.5	9.5	11.2	7.9	11.7	9.5	8.7	9.7	7.9	9.2	6.8
Switzerland	6.9	7.1	2.7	0.3	3.6	4.1	2.0	2.7	6.9	7.3	3.3	2.5	4.1	. . .
United Kingdom	14.9	27.3	14.9	13.9	10.9	16.2	14.5	19.9	11.6	7.6	4.9	3.9	10.3	6.5
United States	8.8	9.3	5.2	5.8	7.4	7.3	8.7	9.2	9.6	6.0	3.8	3.8	6.8	3.5
Arithmetic average non-ERM	**15.9**	**14.7**	**12.8**	**12.6**	**12.4**	**13.7**	**12.4**	**14.4**	**13.6**	**13.6**	**12.4**	**8.1**	**12.1**	**. . .**
Standard deviation	8.5	8.4	7.4	8.9	10.5	8.7	9.4	11.4	10.6	12.3	19.2	7.1	11.7	. . .
Coefficient of variation	0.53	0.57	0.58	0.70	0.85	0.65	0.75	0.80	0.78	0.90	1.56	0.87	0.97	. . .
Of which:														
Central European and Scandinavian Countries[1]														
Average	11.7	10.5	8.1	6.9	6.5	8.7	5.8	8.6	9.6	8.3	6.4	5.9	7.4	. . .
Standard deviation	5.5	3.5	3.8	3.8	2.0	3.3	2.4	4.3	2.9	1.3	2.6	2.0	2.3	. . .
Coefficient of variation	0.47	0.33	0.47	0.55	0.31	0.38	0.41	0.50	0.30	0.16	0.40	0.34	0.31	. . .
Southern European Countries[2]														
Average	18.8	15.1	16.1	20.7	18.5	17.8	18.7	16.5	15.7	20.0	15.5	15.7	16.8	. . .
Standard deviation	1.8	2.0	0.5	5.7	4.0	2.2	1.6	1.8	3.0	4.8	3.6	4.4	3.3	. . .
Coefficient of variation	0.09	0.13	0.03	0.28	0.22	0.12	0.09	0.11	0.19	0.24	0.23	0.28	0.20	. . .
Atlantic Countries[3]														
Average	13.0	15.8	9.9	9.0	8.3	11.2	11.2	13.5	10.6	8.0	4.7	3.6	8.5	. . .
Standard deviation	3.0	8.2	4.0	3.5	1.8	3.8	2.4	4.6	0.8	1.8	0.7	0.4	1.4	. . .
Coefficient of variation	0.23	0.52	0.40	0.39	0.22	0.34	0.22	0.34	0.08	0.22	0.15	0.11	0.16	. . .
Pacific Countries[4]														
Average	14.3	11.8	12.9	10.2	8.7	11.5	9.4	9.9	9.1	8.0	5.0	3.7	5.6	. . .
Standard deviation	6.3	3.3	5.0	4.2	3.7	1.9	6.1	5.2	5.0	4.5	3.3	3.2	3.8	. . .
Coefficient of variation	0.44	0.28	0.38	0.41	0.42	0.16	0.65	0.53	0.55	0.56	0.66	0.86	0.68	. . .

Source: International Monetary Fund, *International Financial Statistics*, various issues.
[1] Austria, Finland, Norway, Sweden, Switzerland.
[2] Greece, Portugal, Spain.
[3] Canada, United Kingdom, United States.
[4] Australia, Japan, New Zealand.

Table 33. Generalized Least Squares Estimates of Inflation Equation for 22 Countries, 1974–84[1]

Endogenous Variable[2]	Exogenous Variables[3]								adj.R^2	F(4,236)	DW
	Constant	gdp_t	$m1_t$	$m1_{t-1}$	$m2_t$	$m2_{t-1}$	delta p_t	dummy			
cp_t	12.4** (6.0)	−0.4** (−5.5)	0.1** (6.4)				0.5** (17.9)	−2.1 (−1.9)	0.63	102.2	1.8
cp_t	13.7** (6.0)	−0.6** (−6.4)		0.7* (2.6)			0.5** (15.9)	2.6* (−2.2)	0.58	82.9	1.8
cp_t	11.1** (6.0)	−0.5** (−6.2)			0.2** (6.0)		0.4** (15.3)	−1.9 (−1.7)	0.62	97.5	1.8
cp_t	12.0** (5.9)	−0.5** (−6.3)				0.2** (4.6)	0.5** (16.6)	−2.1 (−1.8)	0.60	89.7	1.8
wp_t[4]	12.1** (7.6)	−0.6** (−4.9)	0.2** (6.0)				0.6** (20.9)	−4.2** (−2.8)	0.65	111.8	1.9
wp_t[4]	13.4** (7.6)	−0.7** (−5.6)		0.1** (3.3)			0.5** (19.6)	−4.8** (−3.0)	0.62	98.5	1.8
wp_t[4]	10.6** (6.8)	−0.6** (−4.7)			0.3** (5.2)		0.5** (19.1)	−3.8* (−2.5)	0.63	101.8	1.9
wp_t[4]	11.0** (6.9)	−0.6** (−5.4)				0.2** (5.2)	0.5** (19.7)	−4.0* (−2.6)	0.63	103.1	1.8

Source: Fund staff estimates on the basis of *International Financial Statistics* data.

[1] Pooled cross-section and time series analysis. All variables (except dummy) in percentage changes (for the list of sample countries see text).

[2] cp = percentage change of consumer prices, wp = percentage change of wholesale prices.

[3] gdp = percentage change of GDP (or GNP), m1 = percentage change of M1, m2 = percentage change of M2, delta p = change in the rate of inflation (proxy for expected inflation), dummy = dummy variable which takes the value of 1 in 1979–84 for all countries participating in the EMS exchange rate mechanism and 0 otherwise. * and ** indicate statistical significance at the 5 percent and 1 percent level, respectively.

[4] Consumer prices were used in the case of Iceland.

Table 34. Generalized Least Squares Estimates of Inflation Equation for 22 Countries, 1979–84[1]

Endogenous Variable[2]	Exogenous Variables[3]								adj.R^2	$F(4,126)$	DW
	Constant	gdp_t	$m1_1$	$m1_{t-1}$	$m2_t$	$m2_{t-1}$	delta p_t	dummy			
cp_t	11.5** (4.1)	−0.6** (−4.0)	0.3** (4.0)				0.5** (14.5)	−2.3 (−0.7)	0.68	69.6	1.8
cp_t	13.2** (4.0)	−0.7** (−4.0)		0.2** (3.5)			0.5** (11.2)	−3.3 (−0.8)	0.56	42.4	1.8
cp_t	9.0** (3.8)	−0.7** (−4.5)			0.3** (6.8)		0.3** (7.6)	−0.6 (−0.2)	0.63	56.5	1.8
cp_t	10.0** (3.8)	−0.5** (−2.7)				0.3** (5.8)	0.6** (12.8)	−3.1 (−0.9)	0.61	51.8	1.8
wp_t[4]	11.6** (4.2)	−0.5** (−3.1)	0.2** (6.9)				0.5** (15.1)	−3.9 (−1.1)	0.67	66.2	1.6
wp_t[4]	13.9** (3.9)	−0.6** (−3.0)		0.1 (2.0)			0.5** (11.8)	−4.9 (−1.1)	0.56	42.7	1.6
wp_t[4]	8.9** (3.7)	−0.6** (−3.1)			0.3** (6.0)		0.4** (9.9)	−1.7 (−0.5)	0.63	56.1	1.6
wp_t[4]	11.1** (3.8)	−0.4* (−2.2)				0.2** (4.0)	0.6** (13.1)	−4.6 (−1.2)	0.59	47.9	1.6

Source: Fund staff estimates on the basis of *International Financial Statistics* data.

[1] Pooled cross-section and time series analysis. All variables (except dummy) in percentage changes (for the list of sample countries see text).

[2] cp = percentage change of consumer prices, wp = percentage change of wholesale prices.

[3] gdp = percentage change of GDP (or GNP), m1 = percentage change of M1, m2 = percentage change of M2, delta p = change in the rate of inflation (proxy for expected inflation), dummy = dummy variable which takes the value of 1 in 1979–84 for all countries participating in the EMS exchange rate mechanism and 0 otherwise. * and ** indicate statistical significance at the 5 percent and 1 percent level, respectively.

[4] Consumer prices were used in the case of Iceland.

Table 35. Generalized Least Squares Estimates of Inflation Equation for Seven ERM Countries, 1974–84[1]

Endogenous Variable[3]	Exogenous Variables[2]								adj.R²	F(471)	DW
	Constant	gdp_t	$m1_t$	$m1_{t-1}$	$m2_t$	$m2_{t-1}$	delta p_t	dummy			
cp_t	12.1** (6.4)	−0.2* (−2.2)	0.1 (0.2)				0.6** (7.1)	−2.3** (−2.9)	0.46	16.9	1.3
cp_t	12.0** (6.6)	−0.3* (−2.4)		0.0 (0.7)			0.6** (7.4)	−2.3* (−3.0)	0.47	17.1	1.3
cp_t	10.4** (5.8)	−0.2* (−2.3)			0.1* (2.1)		0.6** (7.9)	−1.9* (−2.4)	0.48	18.6	1.3
cp_t	11.2** (5.9)	−0.3* (−2.6)				0.1 (1.3)	0.6** (6.7)	−2.1* (−2.6)	0.47	17.4	1.3
wp_t[4]	13.2** (6.8)	−0.6** (−2.8)	0.0 (−0.3)				0.6** (11.5)	−4.5** (−3.2)	0.68	40.8	1.8
wp_t[4]	12.5** (6.9)	−0.7** (−3.0)		0.1 (1.4)			0.6** (11.6)	−4.3** (−3.2)	0.68	40.1	1.8
wp_t[4]	9.3** (4.5)	−0.7** (−3.1)			0.3** (2.7)		0.6** (11.6)	−3.1* (−2.2)	0.67	38.3	1.8
wp_t[4]	9.9** (4.6)	−0.7** (−3.1)				0.3* (2.2)	0.6** (11.0)	−3.4* (−2.4)	0.67	39.2	1.8

Source: Fund staff estimates on the basis of *International Financial Statistics* data.

[1] Pooled cross-section and time series analysis. All variables (except dummy) in percentage changes (for the list of sample countries see text).

[2] cp = percentage change of consumer prices, wp = percentage change of wholesale prices.

[3] gdp = percentage change of GDP (or GNP), m1 = percentage change of M1, m2 = percentage change of M2, delta p = change in the rate of inflation (proxy for expected inflation), dummy = dummy variable which takes the value of 1 in 1979–84 for all countries participating in the EMS exchange rate mechanism and 0 otherwise. * and ** indicate statistical significance at the 5 percent and 1 percent level, respectively.

[4] Consumer prices were used in the case of Iceland.

Table 36.   Unit Labor Costs, 1974–85

(Annual change in percent)

	1974	1975	1976	1977	1978	Average 1974–78	1979	1980	1981	1982	1983	1984	1985	Average 1979–85
Belgium	15.7	15.2	2.6	5.9	1.3	8.0	3.4	4.0	5.0	3.3	1.8	2.0	2.6	3.1
Denmark	17.2	7.1	7.6	8.4	7.6	9.5	5.7	4.5	8.4	11.3	1.3	−3.2	4.4	4.5
France	14.6	18.8	7.9	6.7	7.2	10.9	9.3	12.4	11.9	11.1	7.6	1.9	1.4	7.9
Germany, Fed. Fep. of	9.0	10.3	0.6	5.3	5.1	6.0	2.3	7.3	5.1	4.1	−0.5	−0.3	−0.1	2.5
Italy	18.8	32.8	10.4	17.5	11.1	17.9	9.6	12.3	19.0	18.2	14.0	3.9	4.5	11.5
Netherlands	10.1	15.6	0.1	4.7	1.7	6.3	2.5	4.0	0.8	4.3	−1.5	−6.7	−1.0	0.3
Arithmetic average ERM	**14.2**	**16.6**	**4.9**	**8.1**	**5.6**	**9.8**	**5.5**	**7.4**	**8.4**	**8.7**	**3.8**	**−0.4**	**2.0**	**5.0**
Standard deviation	3.6	8.2	4.0	4.4	3.4	4.0	3.0	3.6	5.8	5.3	5.4	3.6	2.1	3.7
Coefficient of variation	0.25	0.49	0.81	0.54	0.61	0.41	0.56	0.49	0.70	0.61	1.43	−8.88	1.06	0.74
Austria	10.6	16.6	0.1	5.4	2.7	6.9	−1.2	4.9	5.7	2.5	−0.2	−1.7	2.0	1.7
Canada	13.4	16.1	8.7	7.0	5.3	10.0	7.8	12.9	13.8	13.4	0.4	−4.6	2.3	6.4
Japan	28.5	14.7	−2.4	2.3	−1.8	7.7	−2.1	−2.0	1.8	−1.8	−1.6	−3.7	0.2	−1.3
Norway	13.1	22.4	11.6	12.4	8.0	13.4	0.2	10.8	11.1	6.5	5.1	7.3	5.5	6.6
Sweden	12.9	19.9	16.6	11.2	8.4	13.7	−0.1	9.6	10.2	4.2	0.6	4.0	4.6	4.7
Switzerland	9.6	12.9	−3.9	−2.5	1.6	3.3	−0.8	1.2	7.1	5.3	−1.6	−5.9	1.8	0.9
United Kingdom	18.2	34.4	11.0	14.9	14.8	18.4	17.3	21.6	6.8	4.5	0.2	3.0	5.4	8.2
United States	13.5	8.7	3.3	5.8	7.4	7.7	9.7	11.7	7.3	6.1	−2.8	−1.2	1.7	4.5
Arithmetic average non-ERM	**15.0**	**18.2**	**5.6**	**7.1**	**5.8**	**10.1**	**3.9**	**8.8**	**8.0**	**5.1**	**−0.0**	**−0.3**	**2.9**	**3.9**
Standard deviation	5.6	7.3	6.9	5.3	4.7	4.5	6.5	6.9	3.4	4.0	2.2	4.3	1.8	3.0
Coefficient of variation	0.38	0.40	1.23	0.75	0.82	0.44	1.70	0.78	0.43	0.79	−1,381.19	−12.47	0.63	0.77

Source: International Monetary Fund, *International Financial Statistics*, various issues.

Table 37. Rate of Growth of Narrow Money, 1974–85

(Annual change in percent)

	1974	1975	1976	1977	1978	Average 1974–78	1979	1980	1981	1982	1983	1984	Average 1979–84	1985
Belgium	6.2	15.7	7.0	8.3	5.9	*8.6*	2.5	0.2	2.2	3.9	8.6	0.3	*2.9*	3.2
Denmark	4.7	30.2	6.3	8.0	16.1	*12.7*	9.9	10.9	11.8	13.1	8.5	34.7	*14.5*	27.3
France	15.2	12.6	7.5	11.1	11.1	*11.5*	11.8	6.4	15.9	10.9	12.5	8.9	*11.0*	. . .
Germany, Fed. Rep. of	10.7	14.3	3.3	12.0	14.5	*10.9*	2.9	3.9	−1.5	7.2	8.4	5.9	*4.4*	6.7
Ireland	9.0	19.9	16.9	22.5	27.6	*19.0*	8.1	14.0	3.4	5.4	11.4	9.6	*8.6*	1.9
Italy	9.4	13.5	18.9	21.4	26.6	*17.8*	23.7	12.9	9.8	16.8	13.2	12.4	*14.7*	. . .
Netherlands	12.2	19.7	8.2	13.2	4.2	*11.4*	2.8	6.0	−2.4	9.8	10.1	7.5	*5.5*	6.7
Arithmetic average ERM	**9.6**	**18.0**	**9.7**	**13.8**	**15.1**	*13.1*	**8.8**	**7.8**	**5.6**	**9.6**	**10.4**	**11.3**	*8.8*	. . .
Standard deviation	3.3	5.7	5.4	5.5	8.5	*3.6*	7.0	4.7	6.5	4.2	1.9	10.2	*4.4*	. . .
Difference between highest and lowest value	10.5	17.6	15.6	14.5	23.4	*10.5*	21.2	13.8	18.3	12.9	4.8	34.4	*11.8*	. . .
Coefficient of variation	0.34	0.31	0.55	0.40	0.56	*0.27*	0.79	0.60	1.16	0.43	0.18	0.90	*0.50*	. . .
Weighted average	**11.4**	**14.6**	**7.7**	**13.0**	**14.2**	. . .	**9.1**	**6.4**	**6.3**	**10.3**	**10.7**	**8.9**	. . .	. . .
Australia	−0.7	22.7	8.9	6.6	11.6	*9.6*	15.4	17.5	4.9	−0.2	15.3	8.2	*10.0*	3.6
Austria	5.7	14.3	8.3	1.4	8.3	*7.5*	−9.0	15.6	−2.4	8.2	11.2	3.5	*4.2*	3.1
Canada	1.5	19.0	1.5	10.4	7.0	*7.7*	1.4	10.1	6.2	5.3	10.4	19.7	*8.7*	32.3
Finland	18.9	34.5	−1.7	2.8	16.5	*13.5*	22.5	6.3	14.7	15.9	7.6	16.4	*13.8*	11.0
Greece	19.8	16.4	22.2	16.9	22.3	*19.5*	16.3	16.3	22.2	21.7	14.5	20.2	*18.5*	. . .
Iceland	30.1	33.6	24.7	46.9	40.8	*35.0*	46.5	60.4	61.2	27.5	78.2	107.5	*61.7*	100.6
Japan	11.5	11.1	12.5	8.2	13.4	*11.3*	3.0	−2.0	10.0	5.7	−0.1	6.9	*3.8*	3.0
New Zealand	3.6	9.3	9.2	1.9	22.3	*9.0*	3.4	3.1	15.4	3.5	13.1	9.8	*7.9*	9.1
Norway	11.9	16.6	−3.7	14.1	8.6	*9.3*	7.6	5.3	15.0	12.3	12.1	24.4	*12.6*	20.3
Portugal	10.2	24.5	12.7	11.6	14.2	*14.5*	36.2	13.5	8.9	15.9	7.8	16.6	*16.1*	. . .
Spain	17.3	18.7	21.9	18.5	17.3	*18.7*	8.5	13.5	13.0	11.4	2.3	8.6	*9.5*	. . .
Sweden	13.8	14.1	3.6	10.1	17.1	*11.6*	15.6	18.2	8.0	9.8	. . .	. . .	. . .	. . .
Switzerland	−3.3	4.3	11.7	0.8	23.5	*7.0*	−1.9	−0.1	−5.2	7.0	9.3	0.2	*1.4*	. . .
United Kingdom	10.8	18.6	11.3	20.8	16.3	*15.5*	9.1	4.0	17.7	11.3	11.2	15.5	*11.4*	18.1
United States	4.3	4.9	6.7	8.1	8.3	*6.4*	6.7	6.9	6.4	8.8	9.7	5.7	*7.4*	12.2
Arithmetic average non-ERM	**10.4**	**17.5**	**10.0**	**11.9**	**16.5**	*13.1*	**12.1**	**12.6**	**13.1**	**10.9**	**13.5**	**17.5**	*12.5*	. . .
Standard deviation	8.6	8.1	8.0	11.1	8.3	*7.1*	13.9	14.2	14.6	6.9	18.1	25.5	*14.2*	. . .
Coefficient of variation	0.83	0.49	0.81	0.93	0.50	*0.54*	1.15	1.13	1.12	0.63	1.34	1.45	*1.14*	. . .
Of which:														
Central European and Scandinavian Countries[1]														
Average	7.0	12.3	5.0	6.6	14.4	*8.9*	3.1	9.8	3.9	9.3	10.9	9.4	*6.1*	. . .
Standard deviation	6.7	4.7	5.8	5.7	6.3	*1.8*	9.3	7.5	8.1	2.0	1.2	10.7	*4.8*	. . .
Coefficient of variation	0.95	0.38	1.16	0.86	0.44	*0.20*	3.03	0.76	2.10	0.21	0.11	1.14	*0.78*	. . .
Southern European Countries[2]														
Average	15.8	19.9	18.9	15.7	17.9	*17.6*	20.3	14.4	14.7	16.3	8.2	15.1	*14.7*	. . .
Standard deviation	4.1	3.4	4.4	2.9	3.3	*2.2*	11.7	1.3	5.6	4.2	5.0	4.8	*3.8*	. . .
Coefficient of variation	0.3	0.2	0.2	0.2	0.2	*0.1*	0.6	0.1	0.4	0.3	0.6	0.3	*0.3*	. . .
Atlantic Countries[3]														
Average	5.5	14.2	6.5	13.1	10.5	*9.9*	5.7	7.0	10.1	8.5	10.4	13.6	*9.1*	. . .
Standard deviation	3.9	6.6	4.0	5.5	4.1	*4.0*	3.2	2.5	5.4	2.5	0.6	5.9	*1.7*	. . .
Coefficient of variation	0.70	0.46	0.62	0.42	0.39	*0.41*	0.56	0.36	0.53	0.29	0.06	0.43	*0.18*	. . .
Pacific Countries[4]														
Average	4.8	14.4	10.2	5.6	15.8	*10.0*	7.3	6.2	10.1	3.0	9.4	8.3	*7.3*	. . .
Standard deviation	5.1	5.9	1.6	2.7	4.7	*1.0*	5.8	8.3	4.3	2.4	6.8	1.2	*2.6*	. . .
Coefficient of variation	1.05	0.41	0.16	0.48	0.30	*0.10*	0.79	1.33	0.42	0.81	0.72	0.14	*0.35*	. . .

Source: International Monetary Fund, *International Financial Statistics*, various issues.

[1] Austria, Finland, Norway, Sweden, Switzerland.
[2] Greece, Portugal, Spain.
[3] Canada, United Kingdom, United States.
[4] Australia, Japan, New Zealand.

Table 38.   Rate of Growth of Broad Money, 1974–85

(Annual change in percent)

	1974	1975	1976	1977	1978	Average 1974–78	1979	1980	1981	1982	1983	1984	Average 1979–84	1985
Belgium	8.7	15.3	12.6	8.4	7.5	10.5	6.2	3.3	6.3	7.2	8.3	4.5	6.0	5.3
Denmark	8.4	26.9	11.7	9.3	6.4	12.3	10.2	11.7	10.8	11.1	19.7	25.1	14.6	18.4
France	17.8	15.7	12.3	14.6	12.2	14.5	13.9	8.3	11.1	11.3	11.4	7.9	10.6	...
Germany, Fed. Rep. of	7.2	11.5	7.6	10.3	10.3	9.4	5.2	4.6	3.7	6.9	5.7	5.6	5.3	5.1
Ireland	19.3	21.7	13.0	20.6	23.5	19.6	13.6	20.6	10.8	6.7	6.7	9.0	11.1	5.0
Italy	15.7	24.5	21.0	22.2	23.0	21.2	19.4	12.2	10.2	17.6	13.7	10.8	13.9	...
Netherlands	16.1	12.9	17.1	12.9	11.4	14.1	11.6	5.6	7.8	5.3	5.0	7.6	7.1	7.3
Arithmetic average ERM	**13.3**	**18.4**	**13.6**	**14.0**	**13.5**	**14.5**	**11.4**	**9.5**	**8.7**	**9.5**	**10.1**	**10.1**	**9.8**	**...**
Standard deviation	4.7	5.5	4.0	5.1	6.5	4.1	4.5	5.5	2.6	3.9	4.9	6.4	3.5	...
Difference between highest and lowest value	12.1	15.4	13.4	13.8	17.1	11.9	14.2	17.3	7.4	12.3	14.7	20.6	9.4	...
Coefficient of variation	0.35	0.30	0.29	0.36	0.48	0.28	0.39	0.58	0.30	0.42	0.48	0.64	0.36	...
Weighted average	**12.4**	**15.8**	**12.3**	**13.5**	**12.6**	**...**	**10.7**	**7.3**	**7.8**	**10.3**	**9.4**	**8.0**	**...**	**...**
Australia	9.2	20.6	12.3	5.9	10.5	11.6	11.6	14.0	9.9	10.6	13.2	11.7	11.8	17.9
Austria	12.5	18.4	16.9	9.1	14.3	14.2	8.1	12.8	10.3	11.0	5.2	6.4	8.9	6.0
Canada	14.9	12.8	14.8	11.7	15.1	13.9	12.6	14.1	47.3	5.0	−0.9	5.9	13.0	5.9
Finland	17.6	22.3	9.3	11.4	15.2	15.1	18.1	15.1	15.9	13.4	13.3	15.6	15.2	18.1
Greece	20.4	24.1	24.1	22.6	23.8	23.0	17.3	21.0	31.3	27.0	21.1	25.2	23.7	...
Iceland	28.6	29.0	32.9	44.1	48.4	36.4	57.2	65.3	71.6	58.1	79.2	33.9	60.2	48.4
Japan	11.5	14.5	13.5	11.1	13.1	12.7	8.4	6.8	10.7	7.6	6.9	6.9	7.9	8.9
New Zealand	6.0	10.7	18.3	14.7	24.7	14.7	18.6	9.2	16.4	14.1	6.6	20.4	14.1	32.6
Norway	11.1	15.3	10.5	17.3	12.3	13.3	13.3	11.0	13.5	11.3	11.1	20.4	13.4	14.0
Portugal	13.6	12.6	20.9	16.9	20.8	16.9	37.8	24.6	23.5	23.1	15.5	24.7	24.7	...
Spain	19.1	19.0	19.3	18.7	20.3	19.3	17.9	16.7	15.8	16.1	10.0	10.8	14.5	...
Sweden	9.7	11.7	5.0	9.1	17.4	10.5	17.1	12.2	13.3	8.0	8.4	7.3	11.0	...
Switzerland	−11.9	7.5	9.0	6.8	11.3	4.2	9.5	0.5	8.4	17.7	10.2	8.2	9.0	...
United Kingdom	12.9	7.1	11.6	9.5	14.6	11.1	12.5	18.5	27.8	11.4	13.0	12.3	15.8	11.4
United States	5.4	12.7	13.7	10.6	7.7	10.0	6.2	7.1	4.7	8.7	16.3	9.0	8.6	9.2
Arithmetic average non-ERM	**12.0**	**15.9**	**15.5**	**14.6**	**18.0**	**15.1**	**17.7**	**16.6**	**21.4**	**16.2**	**15.3**	**14.6**	**16.8**	**...**
Standard deviation	8.6	6.0	6.7	9.1	9.4	7.0	12.8	14.2	17.1	12.6	17.8	8.2	12.6	...
Coefficient of variation	0.71	0.38	0.43	0.62	0.52	0.47	0.72	0.86	0.80	0.77	1.17	0.56	0.75	...
Of which:														
Central European and Scandinavian Countries[1]														
Average	7.8	15.0	10.1	10.7	14.1	11.4	13.2	10.3	12.3	12.3	9.6	11.6	11.5	...
Standard deviation	10.2	5.1	3.9	3.6	2.2	3.9	4.0	5.1	2.6	3.2	2.7	5.5	2.5	...
Coefficient of variation	1.31	0.34	0.38	0.33	0.15	0.34	0.30	0.49	0.21	0.26	0.28	0.47	0.22	...
Southern European Countries[2]														
Average	17.7	18.6	21.4	19.4	21.6	19.7	24.3	20.8	23.5	22.1	15.5	20.2	21.0	...
Standard deviation	2.9	4.7	2.0	2.4	1.5	2.5	9.5	3.2	6.3	4.5	4.5	6.7	4.6	...
Coefficient of variation	0.17	0.25	0.09	0.12	0.07	0.13	0.39	0.16	0.27	0.20	0.29	0.33	0.22	...
Atlantic Countries[3]														
Average	11.1	10.9	13.4	10.6	12.5	11.6	10.4	13.2	26.6	8.4	9.5	9.1	12.5	...
Standard deviation	4.1	2.7	1.3	0.9	3.4	1.6	3.0	4.7	17.4	2.6	7.5	2.6	3.0	...
Coefficient of variation	0.37	0.25	0.10	0.08	0.27	0.14	0.29	0.35	0.65	0.31	0.79	0.29	0.24	...
Pacific Countries[4]														
Average	8.9	15.3	14.7	10.6	16.1	13.0	12.9	10.0	12.3	10.8	8.9	13.0	11.3	...
Standard deviation	2.3	4.1	2.6	3.6	6.2	1.3	4.3	3.0	2.9	2.7	3.0	5.6	2.6	...
Coefficient of variation	0.25	0.27	0.18	0.34	0.38	0.10	0.33	0.30	0.23	0.25	0.34	0.43	0.23	...

Source: International Monetary Fund, *International Financial Statistics*, various issues.

[1] Austria, Finland, Norway, Sweden, Switzerland.
[2] Greece, Portugal, Spain.
[3] Canada, United Kingdom, United States.
[4] Australia, Japan, New Zealand.

Table 39. Rate of Growth of Domestic Credit, 1974–85

(Annual change in percent)

	1974	1975	1976	1977	1978	Average 1974–78	1979	1980	1981	1982	1983	1984	Average 1979–84	1985
Belgium	10.6	13.8	16.3	15.2	10.8	*13.3*	14.8	11.5	12.8	10.7	14.3	6.6	*11.7*	9.7
Denmark	10.4	26.7	14.7	3.4	4.2	*11.6*	12.3	13.3	14.5	13.3	22.2	24.7	*16.6*	13.8
France	18.0	18.6	21.0	20.0	8.8	*17.2*	14.1	12.7	13.6	16.1	13.3	−2.5	*11.0*	...
Germany, Fed. Rep. of	8.0	10.1	10.6	10.0	11.4	*10.0*	11.9	9.5	8.8	6.5	6.7	6.0	*8.2*	6.2
Ireland	19.5	18.1	12.9	20.4	30.1	*20.1*	30.4	15.3	15.2	27.3	11.2	12.6	*18.4*	3.8
Italy	23.8	23.5	21.4	16.3	17.4	*20.4*	16.0	16.6	12.7	17.9	14.5	13.5	*15.2*	...
Netherlands	16.5	14.3	19.7	23.1	21.0	*18.9*	17.2	10.4	5.9	4.3	4.6	5.8	*7.9*	5.4
Arithmetic average ERM	**15.3**	**17.9**	**16.7**	**15.5**	**14.8**	*15.9*	**16.7**	**12.8**	**11.9**	**13.7**	**12.4**	**9.5**	*12.7*	...
Standard deviation	5.3	5.3	3.9	6.3	8.1	*3.9*	5.9	2.4	3.1	7.1	5.3	7.9	*3.8*	...
Difference between highest and lowest value	15.8	16.6	10.8	19.7	25.9	*10.4*	18.5	7.1	9.3	23.0	17.6	27.2	*10.5*	...
Coefficient of variation	0.35	0.30	0.23	0.41	0.54	*0.25*	0.35	0.19	0.26	0.52	0.43	0.83	*0.30*	...
Weighted average	**14.3**	**16.0**	**16.6**	**15.0**	**12.1**	...	**13.8**	**12.0**	**11.1**	**11.8**	**10.8**	**5.7**	...	...
Australia	15.8	24.6	17.6	8.2	10.6	*15.2*	14.7	13.1	12.4	3.7	14.6	13.3	*11.9*	29.1
Austria	14.7	14.6	24.9	15.8	13.7	*16.7*	17.5	12.2	10.5	8.2	8.1	9.7	*11.0*	7.8
Canada	18.2	19.5	18.8	17.1	20.9	*18.9*	22.8	11.5	31.9	2.2	19.6	15.2	*18.2*	5.9
Finland	27.9	29.7	10.2	12.6	6.6	*17.0*	18.8	20.6	15.0	20.3	19.6	15.2	*18.2*	...
Greece	23.3	24.6	26.4	26.6	23.1	*24.8*	21.4	21.9	36.1	26.4	18.5	19.8	*23.9*	...
Iceland	71.0	48.5	26.7	29.1	43.5	*42.9*	47.6	67.0	67.2	92.7	86.8	44.8	*66.7*	35.2
Japan	15.1	16.7	13.7	10.6	13.7	*13.9*	8.4	8.4	10.0	8.2	7.5	8.9	*8.6*	8.8
New Zealand	28.8	31.9	24.6	20.4	22.6	*25.6*	14.5	10.5	15.9	15.5	6.4	−3.9	*9.6*	56.4
Norway	10.8	15.5	16.0	21.4	10.5	*14.8*	15.6	10.8	12.7	11.8	11.4	15.9	*13.0*	...
Portugal	21.9	43.2	15.0	31.5	20.9	*26.1*	27.4	8.3	34.2	30.7	25.6	12.1	*22.7*	...
Spain	24.4	22.7	22.7	19.9	16.1	*21.1*	17.4	20.6	22.4	22.3	5.2	12.6	*16.6*	...
Sweden	12.8	13.6	7.8	11.5	19.5	*13.0*	18.2	13.4	18.6	11.2	8.2	14.2	*13.9*	...
Switzerland	−10.4	5.9	7.8	7.5	9.0	*3.7*	8.5	11.7	8.9	21.5	8.0	9.4	*11.2*	...
United Kingdom	17.5	8.1	13.8	6.0	10.0	*11.0*	9.8	14.3	20.6	16.5	13.2	19.1	*15.5*	11.9
United States	8.9	6.6	10.7	12.6	11.1	*10.0*	10.9	7.5	6.5	5.7	12.4	12.6	*9.2*	14.4
Arithmetic average non-ERM	**20.0**	**21.7**	**17.1**	**16.7**	**16.8**	*18.3*	**18.2**	**16.8**	**21.5**	**19.8**	**16.3**	**14.1**	*17.6*	...
Standard deviation	16.4	12.1	6.4	7.7	8.8	*8.9*	9.4	14.1	15.2	21.1	19.8	9.8	*13.9*	...
Coefficient of variation	0.82	0.56	0.38	0.46	0.53	*0.48*	0.52	0.84	0.70	1.07	1.21	0.69	*0.79*	...
Of which:														
Central European and Scandinavian Countries[1]														
Average	11.2	15.9	13.3	13.8	11.9	*13.0*	15.7	13.7	13.1	14.6	11.1	12.9	*13.5*	...
Standard deviation	12.3	7.7	6.5	4.7	4.5	*4.9*	3.8	3.5	3.4	5.3	4.5	2.8	*2.6*	...
Coefficient of variation	1.11	0.49	0.49	0.34	0.38	*0.38*	0.24	0.26	0.26	0.36	0.40	0.22	*0.19*	...
Southern European Countries[2]														
Average	23.2	30.2	21.4	26.0	20.0	*24.0*	22.1	16.9	30.9	26.5	16.4	14.8	*21.0*	...
Standard deviation	1.0	9.2	4.7	4.8	2.9	*2.1*	4.1	6.1	6.1	3.4	8.5	3.5	*3.2*	...
Coefficient of variation	0.04	0.31	0.22	0.18	0.15	*0.09*	0.19	0.36	0.20	0.13	0.51	0.24	*0.15*	...
Atlantic Countries[3]														
Average	14.9	11.4	14.4	11.9	14.0	*13.3*	14.5	11.1	19.7	8.1	8.4	13.3	*12.3*	...
Standard deviation	4.2	5.8	3.3	4.6	4.9	*4.0*	5.9	2.8	10.4	6.1	6.3	4.4	*2.6*	...
Coefficient of variation	0.28	0.51	0.23	0.38	0.35	*0.30*	0.41	0.25	0.53	0.75	0.75	0.33	*0.21*	...
Pacific Countries[4]														
Average	19.9	24.4	18.6	13.1	15.6	*18.3*	12.5	10.7	12.8	9.1	9.5	6.1	*10.0*	...
Standard deviation	6.3	6.2	4.5	5.3	5.1	*5.2*	2.9	1.9	2.4	4.9	3.6	7.3	*1.4*	...
Coefficient of variation	0.32	0.25	0.24	0.40	0.33	*0.29*	0.23	0.18	0.19	0.53	0.38	1.20	*0.14*	...

Source: International Monetary Fund, *International Financial Statistics*, various issues.

[1] Austria, Finland, Norway, Sweden, Switzerland.

[2] Greece, Portugal, Spain.

[3] Canada, United Kingdom, United States.

[4] Australia, Japan, New Zealand.

Table 40. Real Narrow Money Stock, 1974–85[1]

(Annual change in percent)

	1974	1975	1976	1977	1978	Average 1974–78	1979	1980	1981	1982	1983	1984	Average 1979–84	1985
Belgium	−5.7	2.6	−2.0	1.2	1.3	−0.6	−1.9	−6.0	−5.1	−4.4	0.9	−5.7	−3.7	−1.6
Denmark	−9.1	18.8	−2.5	−2.8	5.4	1.5	0.3	−1.3	0.1	2.7	1.5	26.8	4.6	21.6
France	1.3	0.7	−2.0	1.6	1.9	0.7	1.0	−6.5	2.2	−0.8	2.6	1.4	−0.1	...
Germany, Fed. Rep. of	3.5	7.9	−1.0	8.0	11.5	5.9	−1.1	−1.4	−7.4	1.8	4.9	3.5	−0.0	4.4
Ireland	−6.8	−0.8	−0.9	7.8	18.5	3.2	−4.5	−3.5	−14.1	−10.0	0.8	0.9	−5.2	−3.3
Italy	−8.2	−3.0	1.7	3.8	12.9	1.2	7.8	−6.8	−6.8	0.3	−1.2	1.4	−1.0	...
Netherlands	2.4	8.3	−0.8	6.2	0.0	3.2	−1.4	−0.5	−8.5	3.7	7.2	4.0	0.6	4.4
Arithmetic average ERM	**−3.2**	**4.9**	**−1.1**	**3.7**	**7.4**	**2.2**	**0.0**	**−3.7**	**−5.7**	**−1.0**	**2.4**	**4.6**	**−0.7**	...
Standard deviation	5.0	6.9	1.3	3.7	6.5	2.0	3.6	2.5	5.1	4.4	2.6	9.5	2.9	...
Difference between highest and lowest value	12.6	21.8	4.2	10.8	18.5	6.5	12.3	6.3	16.3	13.7	8.4	32.5	9.8	...
Coefficient of variation	−1.6	1.4	−1.2	1.0	0.9	0.9	0.0	−0.7	−0.9	−4.6	1.1	2.1	−4.2	...
Weighted average	**−0.1**	**4.0**	**−0.9**	**4.6**	**7.3**	...	**0.9**	**−4.0**	**−4.2**	**0.6**	**2.9**	**2.8**	...	...
Australia	−13.8	6.7	−4.1	−5.0	3.4	−2.8	5.8	6.7	−4.4	−10.2	4.7	4.0	0.9	−3.0
Austria	−3.5	5.4	0.9	−3.9	4.5	0.6	−12.2	8.7	−8.6	2.6	7.6	−2.0	−1.0	−0.1
Canada	−8.5	7.4	−5.6	2.2	−1.8	−1.4	−7.1	−0.1	−5.5	−5.0	4.3	14.7	−0.1	27.3
Finland	1.9	14.2	−14.1	−8.7	8.0	−0.3	14.0	−4.7	2.4	6.0	−0.7	8.7	4.1	4.9
Greece	−5.6	2.7	7.8	4.3	8.6	3.4	−2.2	−6.8	−1.8	0.6	−4.8	1.4	−2.3	...
Iceland	−9.0	−10.3	−5.7	12.6	−2.3	−3.3	0.7	1.2	7.0	−14.5	−4.3	58.6	6.0	52.0
Japan	−10.4	−0.6	2.9	0.2	9.2	0.1	−0.5	−9.3	4.8	3.0	−1.9	4.5	−0.0	1.0
New Zealand	−6.8	−4.5	−6.8	−10.9	9.2	−4.2	−9.0	−12.0	0.1	−10.9	5.4	3.4	−4.1	−5.4
Norway	2.3	4.4	−11.8	4.6	0.5	−0.2	2.7	−4.9	1.1	0.8	3.4	17.0	3.1	13.8
Portugal	−13.9	3.4	−4.7	−12.2	−7.0	−7.1	10.1	−2.7	−9.3	−5.5	−13.8	−9.5	−5.4	...
Spain	1.4	1.5	6.0	−4.8	−2.1	0.3	−6.2	−1.8	−1.4	−2.6	−8.8	−2.4	−3.9	...
Sweden	3.6	3.9	6.1	1.2	6.6	1.3	7.9	4.0	−3.7	1.1	...	...	...	...
Switzerland	−11.9	−2.3	9.8	−0.4	22.2	2.8	−5.2	−4.0	−11.0	1.3	6.2	−6.3	−3.3	...
United Kingdom	−4.4	−4.6	−4.5	4.3	7.4	−0.5	−3.8	−11.9	5.2	2.5	6.3	10.0	1.1	11.3
United States	−6.0	−3.9	0.9	1.5	0.6	−1.4	−4.1	−5.8	−3.5	2.5	6.3	1.4	−0.6	8.3
Arithmetic average non-ERM	**−5.6**	**1.6**	**−2.3**	**−1.2**	**4.5**	**−0.8**	**−0.6**	**−2.9**	**−1.9**	**−1.9**	**0.7**	**7.4**	**−0.4**	...
Standard deviation	5.6	5.9	6.7	6.4	6.8	2.6	7.2	6.0	5.3	5.8	6.3	15.9	3.2	...
Coefficient of variation	−1.0	3.8	−2.8	−5.5	1.5	−3.1	−11.9	−2.1	−2.8	−3.1	9.0	2.2	−8.1	...
Of which:														
Central European and Scandinavian Countries[2]														
Average	−1.5	5.1	−4.3	−1.9	8.4	0.8	1.4	−0.2	−4.0	2.4	4.1	4.4	0.7	...
Standard deviation	5.7	5.3	8.7	4.4	7.4	1.1	9.3	5.5	5.2	1.9	3.2	9.1	3.0	...
Coefficient of variation	−3.8	1.0	−2.1	−2.3	0.9	1.4	6.4	−30.8	−1.3	0.8	0.8	2.1	4.1	...
Southern European Countries[3]														
Average	−6.0	2.5	3.0	−4.2	−0.2	−1.1	0.6	−3.8	−4.2	−2.5	−9.1	−3.5	−3.9	...
Standard deviation	6.3	0.8	5.5	6.7	6.5	4.4	6.9	2.2	3.6	2.5	3.7	4.5	1.3	...
Coefficient of variation	−1.0	0.3	1.8	−1.6	−39.1	−4.0	12.2	−0.6	−0.9	−1.0	−0.4	−1.3	−0.3	...
Atlantic Countries[4]														
Average	−6.3	−0.4	−3.1	2.7	2.1	−1.1	−5.0	−5.9	−1.3	0.0	5.6	8.7	0.1	...
Standard deviation	1.7	5.5	2.8	1.2	3.9	0.4	1.5	4.8	4.6	3.5	0.9	5.5	0.7	...
Coefficient of variation	−0.3	−15.0	−0.9	0.4	1.9	−0.4	−0.3	−0.8	−3.7	...	0.2	0.6	5.0	...
Pacific Countries[5]														
Average	−5.7	−1.7	−1.3	−3.6	6.1	−1.4	−3.2	−7.1	1.6	−2.6	1.2	2.6	−1.4	...
Standard deviation	2.9	4.6	4.1	4.5	2.7	1.8	6.1	8.3	3.8	6.4	3.3	0.4	2.2	...
Coefficient of variation	−0.5	−2.7	−3.1	−1.3	0.4	−1.3	−1.9	−1.2	2.3	−2.4	2.8	0.2	−1.6	...

Sources: International Monetary Fund, *International Financial Statistics*; and Fund staff calculations.
[1] Deflated by the consumer price index.
[2] Austria, Finland, Norway, Sweden, Switzerland.
[3] Greece, Portugal, Spain.
[4] Canada, United Kingdom, United States.
[5] Australia, Japan, New Zealand.

Table 41. Real Broad Money Stock, 1974–85[1]

(Annual change in percent)

	1974	1975	1976	1977	1978	Average 1974–78	1979	1980	1981	1982	1983	1984	Average 1979–84	1985
Belgium	−3.5	2.2	3.1	1.2	2.9	1.2	1.6	−3.1	−1.2	−1.4	0.6	−1.7	−0.9	0.4
Denmark	−5.8	15.8	2.5	−1.6	−3.3	1.2	0.6	−0.5	−0.8	0.9	12.0	17.7	4.7	13.1
France	3.6	3.5	2.5	4.8	2.9	3.5	2.9	−4.8	−2.0	−0.4	1.7	0.4	−0.4	...
Germany, Fed. Rep. of	0.2	5.2	3.1	6.4	7.4	4.4	1.0	−0.8	−2.5	1.5	2.4	3.1	0.8	2.9
Ireland	2.0	0.7	−4.2	6.1	14.8	3.7	0.3	2.0	−8.0	−8.8	−3.5	0.4	−3.0	−0.4
Italy	−2.9	6.4	3.6	4.5	9.7	4.2	4.0	−7.4	−6.5	1.0	−0.8	0.0	−1.7	...
Netherlands	5.9	2.2	7.4	6.0	6.9	5.7	7.1	−0.8	1.0	−0.6	2.1	4.1	2.1	5.0
Arithmetic average ERM	**−0.1**	**5.1**	**2.6**	**3.9**	**5.9**	*3.4*	**2.5**	**−2.2**	**−2.9**	**−1.1**	**2.1**	**3.4**	*0.2*	...
Standard deviation	3.9	4.7	3.2	2.8	5.3	1.5	2.2	2.9	3.0	3.3	4.5	6.1	2.4	...
Difference between highest and lowest value	11.7	15.1	11.6	8.0	18.1	4.5	6.8	9.4	9.0	10.3	15.5	19.4	7.8	...
Coefficient of variation	−54.5	0.9	1.2	0.7	0.9	0.5	0.9	−1.3	−1.0	−2.9	2.2	1.8	10.4	...
Weighted average	**0.6**	**4.9**	**3.3**	**5.0**	**5.8**	...	**2.5**	**−3.3**	**−2.7**	**0.5**	**1.7**	**2.0**	...	...
Australia	−5.2	4.8	−1.1	−5.7	2.4	−1.0	2.3	3.5	0.2	−0.5	2.8	7.5	2.6	10.5
Austria	2.7	9.2	8.9	3.4	10.3	6.9	4.3	6.1	3.3	5.2	1.8	0.7	3.5	2.7
Canada	3.6	1.9	6.8	3.4	5.6	4.2	3.1	3.5	31.1	−5.3	−6.4	1.6	3.9	1.9
Finland	0.8	3.9	−4.4	−1.1	6.9	1.1	9.8	3.1	3.5	3.8	4.6	8.0	5.4	11.5
Greece	−5.1	9.4	9.5	9.4	10.0	6.5	−1.4	−3.1	5.4	5.0	0.7	5.7	2.0	...
Iceland	−10.1	−13.4	0.5	10.4	3.0	−2.3	8.1	4.3	13.9	6.0	−3.8	2.3	5.0	12.5
Japan	−10.4	2.4	3.8	2.8	8.9	1.3	4.6	−1.1	5.5	4.8	5.0	4.5	3.9	6.7
New Zealand	−4.6	−3.2	1.1	0.3	11.4	0.8	4.3	−6.8	0.9	−1.8	−0.7	13.4	1.4	14.9
Norway	1.5	3.3	1.2	7.4	4.0	3.5	8.1	0.2	−0.1	−0.1	2.5	13.3	3.9	7.9
Portugal	−11.2	−6.5	2.2	−8.1	−1.5	−5.1	11.4	6.8	2.9	0.3	−7.7	−3.3	1.5	...
Spain	2.9	1.7	3.7	−4.7	0.5	0.8	1.9	1.0	1.1	1.5	−1.9	−0.4	0.5	...
Sweden	−0.2	1.7	−4.7	−2.2	6.8	0.2	9.2	−1.3	1.1	−0.5	−0.5	−0.7	1.2	...
Switzerland	−19.7	0.7	7.2	5.4	10.1	0.1	5.7	−3.4	1.7	11.4	7.0	4.0	4.3	...
United Kingdom	−2.6	−13.8	−4.3	−5.5	5.8	−4.3	−0.8	0.4	14.2	2.5	8.0	7.0	5.1	5.0
United States	−5.0	3.2	7.5	3.8	0.1	1.8	−4.6	−5.6	−5.2	2.4	12.7	4.5	0.5	5.5
Arithmetic average non-ERM	**−4.2**	**0.4**	**2.5**	**1.3**	**5.6**	*1.0*	**4.4**	**0.5**	**5.3**	**2.3**	**1.6**	**4.5**	*3.0*	...
Standard deviation	6.3	6.7	4.7	5.5	4.0	3.3	4.4	4.0	8.4	3.8	5.3	4.7	1.6	...
Coefficient of variation	−1.5	18.9	1.8	4.4	0.7	3.4	1.0	7.8	1.6	1.7	3.3	1.0	0.6	...
Of which:														
Central European and Scandinavian Countries[2]														
Average	−3.0	3.8	1.6	2.6	7.6	2.4	7.4	0.9	1.9	4.0	3.1	5.1	3.7	...
Standard deviation	8.4	2.9	5.7	3.7	2.4	2.6	2.1	3.3	1.4	4.3	2.5	5.1	1.4	...
Coefficient of variation	−2.8	0.8	3.5	1.4	0.3	1.1	0.3	3.6	0.7	1.1	0.8	1.0	0.4	...
Southern European Countries[3]														
Average	−4.5	1.5	5.1	−1.1	3.0	0.7	4.0	1.6	3.1	2.3	−3.0	0.7	1.4	...
Standard deviation	5.8	6.5	3.1	7.6	5.0	4.7	5.4	4.1	1.8	2.0	3.5	3.8	0.6	...
Coefficient of variation	−1.3	4.2	0.6	−6.7	1.7	6.8	1.4	2.6	0.6	0.9	−1.2	5.6	0.5	...
Atlantic Countries[4]														
Average	−1.3	−2.9	3.3	0.6	3.8	0.6	−0.8	−0.6	13.4	−0.1	4.8	4.4	3.2	...
Standard deviation	3.6	7.7	5.4	4.3	2.6	3.6	3.1	3.8	14.8	3.7	8.1	2.2	2.0	...
Coefficient of variation	−2.7	−2.7	1.6	7.6	0.7	6.0	−4.1	−6.7	1.1	−27.4	1.7	0.5	0.6	...
Pacific Countries[5]														
Average	−6.7	1.3	1.3	−0.9	7.6	0.4	3.7	−1.5	2.2	0.8	2.4	8.5	2.6	...
Standard deviation	2.6	3.4	2.0	3.6	3.8	1.0	1.0	4.2	2.4	2.9	2.3	3.7	1.0	...
Coefficient of variation	−0.4	2.5	1.6	−4.1	0.5	2.8	0.3	−2.9	1.1	3.4	1.0	0.4	0.4	...

Sources: International Monetary Fund, *International Financial Statistics*; and Fund staff calculations.
[1] Deflated by the consumer price index.
[2] Austria, Finland, Norway, Sweden, Switzerland.
[3] Greece, Portugal, Spain.
[4] Canada, United Kingdom, United States.
[5] Australia, Japan, New Zealand.

Table 42. Real Domestic Credit, 1974–85[1]

(Annual change in percent)

	1974	1975	1976	1977	1978	Average 1974–78	1979	1980	1981	1982	1983	1984	Average 1979–84	1985
Belgium	−1.8	0.9	6.5	7.6	6.0	3.8	9.9	4.6	4.8	1.8	6.2	0.2	4.5	4.6
Denmark	−4.1	15.6	5.3	−7.0	−5.3	0.6	2.5	0.9	2.5	2.9	14.3	17.3	6.5	8.8
France	3.8	6.1	10.4	9.7	−0.2	5.9	3.0	−0.9	0.2	3.8	3.4	−9.3	−0.1	...
Germany, Fed. Rep. of	0.9	3.9	6.0	6.1	8.5	5.0	7.5	3.8	2.3	1.2	3.3	3.5	3.6	3.9
Ireland	2.1	−2.3	−4.3	6.0	20.8	4.1	15.2	−2.5	−4.3	8.7	0.7	3.7	3.4	−1.6
Italy	3.9	5.6	3.9	−0.6	4.7	3.5	1.1	−3.8	−4.4	1.2	−0.2	2.4	−0.7	...
Netherlands	6.3	3.4	9.8	15.5	16.1	10.1	12.5	3.6	−0.8	−1.5	1.8	2.4	2.9	3.1
Arithmetic average ERM	**1.6**	**4.7**	**5.4**	**5.3**	**7.2**	*4.7*	**7.4**	**0.8**	**0.0**	**2.6**	**4.2**	**2.9**	*2.9*	...
Standard deviation	3.3	5.2	4.5	6.7	8.3	2.7	5.0	3.1	3.2	2.9	4.5	7.2	2.3	...
Difference between highest and lowest value	10.4	17.9	14.7	22.5	26.1	9.6	14.1	8.4	9.2	10.2	14.5	26.6	7.2	...
Coefficient of variation	2.1	1.1	0.8	1.3	1.2	0.6	0.7	3.8	75.4	1.1	1.1	2.5	0.8	...
Weighted average	**2.3**	**5.0**	**7.3**	**6.5**	**5.5**	...	**5.5**	**1.0**	**0.3**	**1.8**	**3.0**	**−0.1**	...	...
Australia	0.6	8.3	3.6	−3.6	2.4	2.2	5.2	2.7	2.5	−6.7	4.0	9.0	2.7	21.0
Austria	4.7	5.7	16.4	9.8	9.8	9.2	13.3	5.5	3.4	2.6	4.6	3.8	5.5	4.5
Canada	6.6	7.9	10.5	8.4	10.9	8.8	12.6	1.2	17.3	−7.8	−6.0	3.8	3.1	1.9
Finland	9.6	10.2	−3.6	−0.1	−1.1	2.8	10.5	8.1	2.7	10.0	10.4	7.6	8.2	...
Greece	−2.8	9.9	11.5	12.9	9.4	8.0	2.1	−2.3	9.3	4.5	−1.5	1.1	2.1	...
Iceland	19.6	−0.3	−4.1	−1.1	−0.4	2.4	1.5	5.4	11.0	29.2	0.4	10.7	9.3	2.5
Japan	−7.5	4.4	4.0	2.3	9.5	2.4	4.7	0.4	4.8	5.5	5.6	6.5	4.6	6.6
New Zealand	15.9	15.3	6.4	5.3	9.5	10.4	0.7	−5.7	0.5	−0.6	−0.9	−9.5	−2.7	35.5
Norway	1.2	3.5	6.2	11.3	2.3	4.8	10.3	0.0	−0.9	0.4	2.7	9.0	3.5	...
Portugal	−4.7	18.9	−2.8	3.5	−1.4	2.4	3.1	−7.2	11.8	6.5	0.4	−13.0	−0.1	...
Spain	7.5	4.9	6.7	−3.7	−3.1	2.3	1.5	4.3	6.9	6.9	−6.2	1.2	2.3	...
Sweden	2.6	3.5	−2.3	0.0	8.7	2.4	10.2	−0.2	5.8	2.5	−0.6	5.7	3.8	...
Switzerland	−18.4	−0.8	6.0	6.1	7.8	−0.4	4.8	7.4	2.2	14.6	5.1	6.3	6.7	...
United Kingdom	1.3	−13.1	−2.3	−8.5	1.6	−4.4	−3.2	−3.1	7.8	7.3	8.2	13.5	4.9	5.5
United States	−1.8	−2.4	4.7	5.7	3.2	1.8	−0.4	−5.3	−3.5	−0.4	8.9	8.0	1.1	10.5
Arithmetic average non-ERM	**2.3**	**5.1**	**4.1**	**3.2**	**4.6**	*3.7*	**5.1**	**0.7**	**5.4**	**5.0**	**2.3**	**4.2**	*3.7*	...
Standard deviation	9.0	7.4	5.9	5.9	4.8	3.8	4.9	4.7	5.2	8.6	4.8	6.9	3.0	...
Coefficient of variation	3.9	1.5	1.5	1.8	1.0	1.0	1.0	6.2	1.0	1.7	2.1	1.6	0.8	...
Of which:														
Central European and Scandinavian Countries[2]														
Average	−0.1	4.4	4.5	5.4	5.5	3.8	9.8	4.2	2.6	6.0	4.4	6.5	5.5	...
Standard deviation	9.6	3.6	7.2	4.8	4.2	3.2	2.8	3.6	2.2	5.4	3.6	1.8	1.8	...
Coefficient of variation	−160.0	0.8	1.6	0.9	0.8	0.8	0.3	0.9	0.8	0.9	0.8	0.3	0.3	...
Southern European Countries[3]														
Average	0.0	11.2	5.1	4.2	1.6	4.2	2.2	−1.7	9.3	6.0	−2.4	−3.6	1.5	...
Standard deviation	5.4	5.8	5.9	6.8	5.5	2.7	0.7	4.7	2.0	1.0	2.8	6.7	1.1	...
Coefficient of variation	...	0.5	1.2	1.6	3.4	0.6	0.3	−2.7	0.2	0.2	−1.1	−1.9	0.7	...
Atlantic Countries[4]														
Average	2.0	−2.5	4.3	1.9	5.2	2.1	3.0	−2.4	7.2	−0.3	3.7	8.4	3.0	...
Standard deviation	3.5	8.6	5.2	7.4	4.1	5.4	6.9	2.7	8.5	6.2	6.9	4.0	1.6	...
Coefficient of variation	1.7	−3.4	1.2	4.0	0.8	2.6	2.3	−1.1	1.2	−20.5	1.9	0.5	0.5	...
Pacific Countries[5]														
Average	3.0	9.3	4.7	1.3	7.1	5.0	3.5	−0.9	2.6	−0.6	2.9	2.0	1.5	...
Standard deviation	9.7	4.5	1.2	3.7	3.3	3.8	2.0	3.5	1.8	5.0	2.8	8.2	3.1	...
Coefficient of variation	3.2	0.5	0.3	2.8	0.5	0.8	0.6	−4.1	0.7	−8.3	1.0	4.1	2.0	...

Sources: International Monetary Fund, *International Financial Statistics*; and Fund staff calculations.
[1] Deflated by the consumer price index.
[2] Austria, Finland, Norway, Sweden, Switzerland.
[3] Greece, Portugal, Spain.
[4] Canada, United Kingdom, United States.
[5] Australia, Japan, New Zealand.

Table 43.   Short-Term Interest Rates, 1974–85[1]

(Monthly averages in percent)

	1974	1975	1976	1977	1978	Average 1974–78	1979	1980	1981	1982	1983	1984	Average 1979–84	1985
Belgium	9.3	4.6	8.3	5.5	5.2	6.6	8.0	11.2	11.5	11.4	8.2	9.5	10.0	8.3
Denmark	13.3	6.5	10.3	14.5	15.4	12.0	12.6	16.9	14.8	16.4	12.0	11.5	14.0	10.0
France	12.9	7.9	8.6	9.1	8.0	9.3	9.0	11.8	15.3	14.9	12.5	11.7	12.5	9.9
Germany, Fed. Rep. of	8.9	4.4	3.9	4.1	3.4	4.9	5.9	9.1	11.3	8.7	5.4	5.5	7.7	5.2
Ireland	11.3	10.0	10.8	7.7	8.4	9.6	13.5	15.4	13.5	13.2	10.1	8.7	12.4	...
Italy	14.6	10.6	15.7	14.0	11.5	13.3	11.9	17.2	19.6	20.2	18.5	17.3	17.5	15.2
Netherlands	9.2	4.2	7.3	3.8	6.2	6.1	9.0	10.1	11.0	8.1	5.3	5.8	8.2	6.3
Arithmetic average ERM	**11.4**	**6.9**	**9.3**	**8.4**	**8.3**	8.8	**10.0**	**13.1**	**13.9**	**13.3**	**10.3**	**10.0**	11.8	...
Standard deviation	2.1	2.5	3.4	4.1	3.8	2.9	2.5	3.1	2.8	4.0	4.3	3.7	3.2	...
Difference between highest and lowest value	5.7	6.4	11.8	10.7	12.0	8.3	7.6	8.1	8.6	12.1	13.2	11.8	9.8	...
Coefficient of variation	0.19	0.36	0.36	0.49	0.45	0.33	0.26	0.24	0.20	0.30	0.42	0.37	0.27	...
Weighted average	**11.2**	**6.6**	**7.9**	**7.5**	**6.7**	...	**8.4**	**11.8**	**14.1**	**13.0**	**10.3**	**10.1**	...	...
Japan	12.5	10.7	7.0	5.7	4.4	8.1	5.9	10.9	7.4	6.9	6.4	6.1	7.3	6.5
Norway	8.1	7.5	7.4	9.8	9.4	8.4	8.4	11.2	12.3	13.9	12.3	12.7	11.8	...
Sweden	7.5	7.8	7.9	10.0	7.2	8.1	8.2	12.2	14.4	13.3	10.9	11.8	11.8	13.8
United Kingdom	11.4	10.2	11.1	7.7	8.5	9.8	13.0	15.1	13.0	11.5	9.6	9.3	11.9	11.6
United States	10.5	5.8	5.0	5.5	7.9	6.9	11.2	13.4	16.4	12.3	9.1	10.2	12.1	8.1
Arithmetic average non-ERM	**10.0**	**8.4**	**7.7**	**7.7**	**7.5**	8.3	**9.3**	**12.6**	**12.7**	**11.6**	**9.7**	**10.0**	11.0	...
Standard deviation	1.9	1.8	2.0	1.9	1.7	0.9	2.5	1.5	3.0	2.5	2.0	2.3	1.9	...
Coefficient of variation	0.19	0.22	0.26	0.25	0.23	0.11	0.27	0.12	0.24	0.21	0.20	0.23	0.17	...

Source: International Monetary Fund, *International Financial Statistics*, various issues.
[1] In general call money rates, 3-month treasury bill rates for the United Kingdom.

Table 44. Long-Term Interest Rates, 1974–85[1]

(Monthly averages in percent)

	1974	1975	1976	1977	1978	Average 1974–78	1979	1980	1981	1982	1983	1984	Average 1979–84	1985
Belgium	8.7	8.5	9.1	8.8	8.4	*8.7*	9.5	12.0	13.7	13.6	11.9	12.0	*12.1*	10.6
Denmark	14.5	13.1	13.2	13.4	14.5	*13.7*	15.8	17.7	18.9	20.4	14.5	13.9	*16.9*	. . .
France	10.5	9.5	9.2	9.6	9.0	*9.6*	9.5	13.0	15.7	15.6	13.6	12.4	*13.3*	. . .
Germany, Fed. Rep. of	10.4	8.5	7.8	6.2	5.8	*7.7*	7.4	8.5	10.4	9.0	7.9	7.8	*8.5*	6.9
Ireland	16.9	14.6	15.5	11.3	12.8	*14.2*	15.1	15.3	17.3	17.1	13.9	14.6	*15.6*	12.6
Italy	9.9	11.5	13.1	14.6	13.7	*12.6*	14.0	16.1	20.6	20.9	18.0	14.9	*17.4*	. . .
Netherlands	9.8	8.8	8.9	8.1	7.7	*8.7*	8.8	10.2	11.6	10.1	8.6	8.3	*9.6*	7.3
Arithmetic average ERM	**11.5**	**10.6**	**11.0**	**10.3**	**10.3**	*10.7*	**11.4**	**13.3**	**15.5**	**15.2**	**12.6**	**12.0**	*13.3*	. . .
Standard deviation	2.8	2.3	2.7	2.8	3.1	*2.5*	3.2	3.1	3.5	4.3	3.3	2.7	*3.2*	
Difference between highest and lowest value	8.2	6.1	7.7	8.4	8.7	*6.5*	8.4	9.2	10.2	11.9	10.1	7.1	*8.9*	. . .
Coefficient of variation	0.24	0.21	0.25	0.27	0.30	*0.23*	0.28	0.23	0.23	0.28	0.26	0.22	*0.24*	. . .
Weighted average	**10.3**	**9.5**	**9.4**	**9.1**	**8.6**	. . .	**9.6**	**11.8**	**14.4**	**13.8**	**12.0**	**11.0**	. . .	. . .
Australia	9.1	9.8	10.2	10.3	9.1	*9.7*	9.8	11.6	14.0	15.3	14.3	13.8	*13.1*	14.1
Austria	9.7	9.6	8.8	8.7	8.2	*9.0*	8.0	9.2	10.6	9.9	8.2	8.0	*9.0*	7.8
Canada	8.9	9.0	9.2	8.7	9.3	*9.0*	10.2	12.5	15.2	14.3	11.8	12.8	*12.8*	11.0
Japan	9.3	9.2	8.7	7.3	6.1	*8.1*	7.7	9.2	8.7	8.1	7.4	6.8	*8.0*	6.3
New Zealand	6.1	6.3	8.3	9.2	10.0	*8.0*	12.0	13.3	12.8	12.9	12.2	12.6	*12.6*	17.7
Norway	7.1	7.3	7.3	7.4	8.4	*7.5*	8.6	. . .	12.3	13.2	12.9	12.2	*9.9*	. . .
Portugal	. . .	. . .	9.7	10.8	16.2	*7.3*	16.7	16.7	16.7	16.8	. . .	21.5	*14.7*	. . .
Sweden	7.8	8.8	9.3	9.7	10.1	*9.1*	10.5	11.7	13.5	13.0	12.3	12.3	*12.2*	12.3
Switzerland	7.1	6.4	5.0	4.1	3.3	*5.2*	3.4	4.8	5.6	4.8	4.5	4.7	*4.6*	4.7
United Kingdom	14.8	14.4	14.4	12.7	12.5	*13.8*	13.0	13.8	14.7	12.9	10.8	10.7	*12.7*	10.6
United States	8.1	8.2	7.9	7.7	8.5	*8.1*	9.3	11.4	13.7	12.9	11.3	12.5	*11.9*	11.0
Arithmetic average non-ERM	**8.8**	**8.9**	**9.0**	**8.8**	**9.2**	*8.6*	**9.9**	**11.4**	**12.5**	**12.2**	**9.6**	**11.6**	*11.0*	. . .
Standard deviation	2.3	2.2	2.2	2.1	3.1	*2.0*	3.2	3.0	3.0	3.2	4.1	4.2	*2.8*	. . .
Coefficient of variation	0.26	0.25	0.24	0.24	0.34	*0.23*	0.32	0.27	0.24	0.27	0.42	0.36	*0.25*	. . .

Source: International Monetary Fund, *International Financial Statistics*, various issues.

[1] Long-term government bond yields.

Table 45. Matrix of Correlation Coefficients Between Short-Term Interest Rates, January 1974–March 1979 and April 1979–September 1985[1]

	Belgium	Denmark	France	Germany	Italy
Denmark	0.33				
	0.56				
France	0.63	0.34			
	0.53	0.47			
Germany, Fed. Rep. of	0.47	0.10	0.84		
	0.67	0.52	0.66		
Italy	0.58	0.25	0.48	0.25	
	0.46	0.28	0.79	0.48	
Netherlands	0.69	0.29	0.46	0.39	0.25
	0.54	0.46	0.43	0.85	0.10

Source: International Monetary Fund, *International Financial Statistics*, various issues.

[1] For every country, line 1 indicates the correlation coefficient for the five-year period (January 1974–March 1979) prior to the introduction of the EMS and line 2 indicates the correlation coefficient for the seven-year period from April 1979 to September 1985.

Table 46. Matrix of Correlation Coefficients Between Long-Term Interest Rates, January 1974–March 1979 and April 1979–September 1985[1]

	Belgium	Denmark	France	Germany	Ireland	Italy
Denmark	−0.19					
	0.63					
France	0.28	−0.06				
	0.95	0.67				
Germany, Fed. Rep. of	0.14	0.04	0.61			
	0.75	0.68	0.78			
Ireland	0.54	−0.29	0.39	0.63		
	0.61	0.78	0.61	0.78		
Italy	0.33	−0.10	−0.34	−0.83	−0.25	
	0.83	0.74	0.93	0.76	0.63	
Netherlands	0.28	0.05	0.56	0.89	0.59	−0.63
	0.66	0.79	0.71	0.94	0.79	0.72

Source: International Monetary Fund, *International Financial Statistics*, various issues.

[1] For every country, line 1 indicates the correlation coefficient for the five-year period (January 1974–March 1979) prior to the introduction of the EMS and line 2 indicates the correlation coefficient for the seven-year period from April 1979 to September 1985.

Table 47. Central Government Budget Balance as a Ratio of GDP, 1974–84

(In percent)

	1974	1975	1976	1977	1978	Average 1974–78	1979	1980	1981	1982	1983	1984	Average 1979–84
Belgium	−2.8	−4.7	−5.1	−5.9	−6.0	−4.9	−6.5	−8.6	−13.1	−13.8	−13.7	−12.0	−11.3
Denmark	0.7	−2.0	−0.4	−1.3	−0.3	−0.7	−0.7	−2.7	−6.0	−8.5	−7.2	−4.6	−5.0
France	0.5	−2.6	−1.0	−1.2	−1.4	−1.1	−1.5	0.0	−2.8	−3.1	−3.6	−3.3	−2.4
Germany, Fed. Rep. of	−0.7	−3.6	−2.8	−2.1	−2.1	−2.3	−2.0	−1.8	−2.3	−1.9	−2.0	−1.6	−1.9
Ireland	−11.7	−13.2	−10.6	−9.8	−12.8	−11.6	−13.5	−13.7	−15.8	−15.3	−12.5	−11.2	−13.7
Italy	−8.1	−13.1	−9.5	−11.9	−15.4	−11.6	−11.2	−10.9	−13.3	−15.4	−16.4	−15.6	−13.8
Netherlands	−0.6	−3.1	−3.6	−2.9	−3.1	−2.7	−4.1	−4.5	−5.8	−7.3	−8.0	−7.6	−6.2
Arithmetic average ERM	**−3.2**	**−6.0**	**−4.7**	**−5.0**	**−5.9**	**−5.0**	**−5.6**	**−6.0**	**−8.4**	**−9.3**	**−9.1**	**−8.0**	**−7.8**
Standard deviation	4.4	4.6	3.7	4.0	5.5	4.4	4.6	4.7	5.1	5.2	4.9	4.8	4.7
Difference between highest and lowest value	12.4	11.2	10.2	10.7	15.1	11.0	12.8	13.7	13.5	13.5	14.4	14.0	11.9
Coefficient of variation	−1.37	−0.76	−0.78	−0.80	−0.94	−0.88	−0.82	−0.78	−0.60	−0.56	−0.55	−0.60	−0.61
Australia	−1.1	−6.2	−5.3	−2.9	−3.5	−3.8	−2.9	−1.9	−0.9	−0.6	−4.4	−4.0	−2.4
Austria	−1.9	−4.7	−4.7	−3.7	−4.2	−3.8	−3.4	−3.1	−2.6	−4.1	−5.3	−4.5	−3.8
Canada	−1.1	−3.7	−2.5	−4.2	−4.4	−3.2	−3.8	−3.3	−2.7	−6.1	−6.7	−6.8	−4.9
Finland	1.0	−2.2	−0.2	−1.0	−1.6	−0.8	−2.8	−2.1	−1.2	−2.1	−3.1	−1.1	−2.1
Greece	−3.2	−3.9	−3.8	−3.7	−3.6	−3.6	−3.6	−3.1	−8.6	−6.8	−9.2	−9.3	−6.8
Japan	−1.3	−4.8	−2.0	−6.2	−6.6	−4.2	−6.2	−6.3	−6.0	−6.0	−5.8	−5.6	−6.0
New Zealand	−4.1	−10.2	−4.4	−5.1	−8.6	−6.5	−5.3	−6.3	−7.2	−7.4	−9.2	−6.9	−7.1
Switzerland	−0.6	−1.3	−1.0	−0.9	−0.0	−0.8	−1.5	−0.0	−0.8	0.5	−0.7	−0.4	−0.5
United Kingdom	−4.2	−7.7	−5.3	−3.0	−4.9	−5.0	−5.3	−4.7	−4.1	−2.8	−4.8	−3.2	−4.2
United States	−0.8	−4.9	−3.3	−2.7	−2.1	−2.8	−1.2	−2.7	−2.5	−4.3	−5.8	−5.1	−3.6
Arithmetic average non-ERM	**−1.7**	**−5.0**	**−3.2**	**−3.3**	**−4.0**	**−3.4**	**−3.6**	**−3.4**	**−3.7**	**−4.0**	**−5.5**	**−4.7**	**−4.1**
Standard deviation	1.6	2.5	1.7	1.6	2.3	1.7	1.5	1.9	2.6	2.5	2.4	2.6	2.0
Coefficient of variation	−0.91	−0.50	−0.53	−0.47	−0.59	−0.48	−0.43	−0.55	−0.71	−0.64	−0.44	−0.54	−0.48

Sources: International Monetary Fund, *International Financial Statistics,* various issues, *World Economic Outlook*, various issues; and Fund staff estimates.

Table 48. Balance of Payments Current Account, 1974–84

(In billions of U.S. dollars)

	1974	1975	1976	1977	1978	Average 1974–78	1979	1980	1981	1982	1983	1984	Average 1979–84
Belgium	0.8	0.2	0.4	−0.6	−0.8	—	−3.1	−4.9	−4.2	−2.6	−0.4	0.2	−2.5
Denmark	−1.0	−0.5	−1.9	−1.7	−1.5	−1.3	−3.0	−2.5	−1.9	−2.3	−1.2	−1.6	−2.1
France	−3.9	2.7	−3.4	−0.4	7.1	0.4	5.1	−4.2	−4.8	−12.1	−5.2	−0.9	−3.7
Germany, Fed. Rep. of	10.3	4.1	3.9	4.1	9.2	6.3	−6.3	−16.0	−5.4	3.2	4.2	6.1	−2.4
Ireland	−0.7	−0.1	−0.4	−0.5	−0.9	−0.5	−2.1	−2.1	−2.6	−1.9	−1.2	−0.9	−1.8
Italy	−8.1	−0.6	−2.9	2.4	6.2	−0.6	5.4	−9.8	−8.6	−5.7	0.6	−2.9	−3.5
Netherlands	2.2	2.0	2.7	1.1	−1.7	1.3	−2.1	−3.0	2.9	3.7	3.9	4.9	1.7
Arithmetic average ERM	**−0.1**	**1.1**	**−0.2**	**0.6**	**2.5**	**0.8**	**−0.9**	**−6.1**	**−3.5**	**−2.5**	**0.1**	**0.7**	**−2.0**
Standard deviation	5.3	1.7	2.6	1.9	4.4	2.4	4.1	4.7	3.3	5.0	3.0	3.2	1.7
Difference between highest and lowest value	18.4	4.7	7.3	5.8	10.9	7.6	11.7	13.9	11.5	15.8	9.4	9.0	5.4
Coefficient of variation	−92.1	1.5	−11.2	3.0	1.8	3.0	−4.7	−0.8	−0.9	−2.0	30.1	4.5	−0.8
Accumulated balance	−0.4	7.8	−1.6	4.4	17.6	5.6	−6.1	−42.5	−24.6	−17.7	0.7	4.9	−14.2
Australia	−2.8	−1.0	−1.9	−3.1	−4.5	−2.7	−2.6	−4.1	−8.2	−8.2	−5.9	−8.3	−6.2
Austria	−0.2	−0.2	−1.1	−2.2	−0.7	−0.9	−1.1	−1.7	−1.5	0.6	0.2	−0.6	−0.7
Canada	−1.5	−4.7	−4.2	−4.1	−4.3	−3.8	−4.1	−1.0	−5.1	2.1	1.4	1.9	−0.8
Finland	−1.2	−2.1	−1.1	−0.1	0.7	−0.8	−0.2	−1.4	−0.4	−0.8	−0.9	—	−0.6
Greece	−1.1	−0.9	−0.9	−1.1	−1.0	−1.0	−1.9	−2.2	−2.4	−1.9	−1.9	−2.1	−2.1
Iceland	−0.2	−0.1	—	—	—	−0.1	—	−0.1	−0.1	−0.3	−0.1	−0.1	0.1
Japan	−4.7	−0.7	3.7	10.9	17.5	5.3	−8.8	−10.8	4.8	6.9	20.8	35.0	8.0
New Zealand	−1.8	−1.2	−0.8	−0.7	−0.5	−1.0	−0.8	−0.8	−1.4	−1.5	−1.1	−1.4	−1.2
Norway	−1.1	−2.5	−3.7	−5.0	−2.1	−2.9	−1.0	1.1	2.2	0.7	2.0	3.2	1.4
Portugal	−0.8	−0.8	−1.3	−1.0	−0.5	−0.9	−0.1	−1.1	−2.6	−3.3	−1.0	−0.5	−1.4
Spain	−3.2	−3.5	−4.3	−2.1	1.6	−2.3	1.1	−5.2	−5.0	−4.2	−2.7	2.3	−2.3
Sweden	−0.6	−0.3	−1.6	−2.2	−0.3	−1.0	−2.4	−4.4	−2.8	−3.3	−0.9	0.4	−2.2
Switzerland	0.2	2.3	3.1	3.4	3.8	2.6	1.3	−1.6	1.5	3.9	1.2	4.0	1.7
United Kingdom	−7.7	−3.5	−1.5	0.1	2.2	−2.1	−1.4	7.5	13.1	6.9	4.7	1.4	5.4
United States	1.9	18.1	4.2	−14.5	−15.5	−1.2	−1.0	1.8	6.4	−8.0	−46.1	−107.4	−25.7
Arithmetic average non-ERM	**−1.7**	**−0.1**	**−0.8**	**−1.4**	**−0.2**	**−0.8**	**−1.5**	**−1.6**	**−0.1**	**−0.7**	**−2.0**	**−5.1**	**−1.9**
Standard deviation	2.2	5.1	2.5	5.0	6.4	2.2	2.4	3.8	5.1	4.4	13.1	28.4	7.0
Coefficient of variation	−1.3	−69.9	−3.3	−3.5	−26.6	−2.6	−1.5	−2.4	. . .	−6.3	−6.5	−5.6	−3.7
Accumulated balance	−24.8	−1.1	−11.4	−21.7	−3.6	−12.5	−23.0	−24.0	−1.5	−10.4	−30.3	−71.5	−26.2

Source: International Monetary Fund, *International Financial Statistics*, various issues.

Table 49.   Real Rates of Growth of Gross Domestic Product, 1974–85

(Annual change in percent)

	1974	1975	1976	1977	1978	Average 1974–78	1979	1980	1981	1982	1983	1984	Average 1979–84	1985
Belgium	4.2	−1.4	5.5	0.3	3.0	2.3	1.6	3.4	−1.5	1.1	0.0	1.5	1.0	0.9
Denmark	−0.9	−0.7	6.5	1.6	1.5	1.6	3.5	−0.4	−0.9	3.0	2.1	3.5	1.8	2.7
France	3.2	0.2	5.2	3.0	3.8	3.1	3.3	1.0	0.5	1.8	0.7	1.6	1.5	1.3
Germany, Fed. Rep. of	0.2	−1.4	5.6	2.7	3.3	2.1	4.0	1.5	0.0	−1.0	1.6	2.7	1.5	2.3
Ireland	4.1	2.3	1.4	8.2	7.2	4.6	3.1	3.1	2.6	0.8	0.0	4.4	2.3	...
Italy	4.1	−3.6	5.9	1.9	2.7	2.1	4.9	3.9	0.2	−0.5	−0.4	2.6	1.8	...
Netherlands	4.0	−1.0	5.4	2.3	2.1	2.5	2.5	0.8	−0.7	−1.7	1.3	1.7	0.6	2.0
Arithmetic average ERM	**2.7**	**−0.8**	**5.1**	**2.9**	**3.4**	**2.6**	**3.3**	**1.9**	**0.0**	**0.5**	**0.8**	**2.6**	**1.5**	...
Standard deviation	2.0	1.7	1.5	2.3	1.7	0.9	1.0	1.5	1.2	1.5	0.9	1.0	0.5	...
Difference between highest and lowest value	5.1	5.9	5.1	7.9	5.7	3.0	3.3	4.3	4.1	4.7	2.5	2.9	1.7	...
Coefficient of variation	0.7	−2.1	0.3	0.8	0.5	0.4	0.3	0.8	43.1	3.1	1.1	0.4	0.3	...
Australia	1.4	2.2	4.2	2.6	3.5	2.8	3.5	1.9	3.6	0.7	0.4	6.8	2.8	4.7
Austria	3.9	−0.4	4.6	4.4	0.5	2.6	4.7	3.0	−0.1	1.2	2.1	2.0	2.1	2.9
Canada	3.6	1.2	5.8	2.0	3.6	3.2	3.2	1.1	3.3	−4.4	3.3	4.7	1.8	...
Finland	3.0	1.1	0.3	0.2	2.6	1.4	7.4	5.6	1.8	2.9	2.9	3.0	3.9	3.0
Greece	−3.6	6.1	6.4	3.4	6.7	3.7	3.7	1.7	−0.3	−0.2	0.4	2.8	1.3	2.1
Iceland	3.5	−2.2	2.8	11.6	5.9	4.2	5.0	−4.2	1.6	−1.5	−5.5	2.7	−0.4	...
Japan	−1.2	2.4	5.3	5.3	5.1	3.3	5.2	4.8	4.0	3.3	3.4	5.8	4.4	...
New Zealand	4.0	3.4	2.1	−5.6	0.0	0.7	2.7	0.7	4.4	−0.2	1.6	3.9	2.2	...
Norway	5.2	4.2	6.8	3.6	4.5	4.9	5.1	4.3	0.9	0.3	4.5	5.6	3.4	4.2
Portugal	1.1	−4.3	6.9	5.7	3.2	2.4	4.5	5.5	5.1	3.8	0.0	−1.7	2.8	...
Spain	5.7	1.1	3.0	3.3	1.8	3.0	0.2	1.5	0.3	1.0	2.5	2.3	1.3	...
Sweden	3.2	2.6	1.1	−1.6	1.8	1.4	3.8	1.7	−0.3	0.8	2.4	3.4	2.0	2.3
Switzerland	1.5	−7.3	−1.4	2.4	0.4	−0.9	2.5	4.6	1.5	−1.1	0.7	2.0	1.7	3.2
United Kingdom	−1.1	−0.7	3.8	1.0	3.8	1.3	2.2	−2.3	−1.2	1.2	3.6	2.0	0.9	3.0
United States	−0.6	−1.2	5.4	5.5	5.0	2.8	2.8	−0.3	2.5	−2.1	3.7	6.8	2.2	2.2
Arithmetic average non-ERM	**2.0**	**0.5**	**3.8**	**2.9**	**3.2**	**2.5**	**3.8**	**2.0**	**1.8**	**0.4**	**1.7**	**3.5**	**2.2**	...
Standard deviation	2.6	3.3	2.4	3.7	2.0	1.4	1.6	2.7	1.9	2.1	2.3	2.2	1.2	...
Coefficient of variation	1.3	6.0	0.6	1.3	0.6	0.6	0.4	1.4	1.0	5.4	1.4	0.6	0.5	...

Source: International Monetary Fund, *International Financial Statistics*, various issues.

Table 50. Gross Fixed Capital Formation, 1974–85

(In percent of GDP)

	1974	1975	1976	1977	1978	Average 1974–78	1979	1980	1981	1982	1983	1984	Average 1979–84	1985
Belgium	22.3	22.1	21.5	21.4	21.2	*21.7*	20.4	20.7	17.8	16.9	15.9	15.6	. . .	. . .
Denmark	24.0	21.1	23.0	22.1	21.7	*22.4*	20.9	18.8	15.6	16.1	15.9	17.3	*17.4*	19.2
France	24.3	23.3	23.3	22.3	21.4	*22.9*	21.5	21.9	21.4	20.8	19.8	18.9	*20.7*	18.8
Germany, Fed. Rep. of	21.6	20.4	20.1	20.2	20.7	*20.6*	21.8	22.7	21.8	20.5	20.6	20.3	*21.3*	19.6
Ireland	25.3	23.3	24.9	24.8	27.6	*25.2*	30.7	29.0	29.0	25.7	22.6	21.0	*26.3*	. . .
Italy	22.4	20.6	20.0	19.6	18.7	*20.3*	18.8	19.8	20.2	19.0	18.0	17.9	*19.0*	. . .
Netherlands	21.9	21.1	19.4	21.1	21.3	*21.0*	21.0	21.0	19.2	18.2	18.1	18.4	*19.3*	18.4
Arithmetic average ERM	**23.1**	**21.7**	**21.7**	**21.6**	**21.8**	**22.0**	**22.2**	**22.0**	**20.7**	**19.6**	**18.7**	**19.0**	**20.7**	. . .
Standard deviation	1.3	1.1	1.9	1.6	2.5	*1.6*	3.6	3.1	3.9	3.0	2.3	1.3	*2.8*	. . .
Difference between highest and lowest value	3.7	2.9	5.5	5.2	8.9	*4.9*	11.9	10.2	13.4	9.6	6.7	3.7	*8.9*	. . .
Coefficient of variation	0.06	0.05	0.09	0.07	0.12	*0.07*	0.16	0.14	0.19	0.15	0.12	0.07	*0.14*	. . .
Australia	22.8	23.2	24.1	25.0	24.6	*23.9*	24.4	25.1	26.9	26.1	23.5	22.6	*24.8*	23.5
Austria	28.4	26.7	26.0	26.7	25.6	*26.7*	25.1	25.5	25.2	23.1	22.2	21.8	*23.8*	22.1
Canada	22.9	23.8	23.0	22.5	22.0	*22.8*	22.4	22.6	23.3	21.4	19.3	18.3	*21.2*	. . .
Finland	29.8	31.3	28.0	27.0	24.0	*28.0*	23.2	25.3	25.0	24.9	24.6	23.4	*24.4*	. . .
Greece	22.2	20.8	21.2	23.0	23.9	*22.2*	25.8	24.2	22.3	20.2	20.3	18.6	*21.9*	19.1
Iceland	31.6	32.2	28.5	27.9	25.4	*29.1*	24.5	25.3	24.8	25.1	22.5	22.2	*24.1*	. . .
Japan	34.8	32.4	31.3	30.5	30.8	*32.0*	32.1	32.0	31.0	29.9	28.5	28.1	*30.3*	. . .
New Zealand	25.9	27.0	24.8	22.4	20.8	*24.2*	18.2	18.2	21.2	23.0	22.7	21.5	*20.8*	. . .
Norway	30.5	34.2	36.3	37.1	31.8	*34.0*	27.7	24.8	28.0	25.5	25.7	26.0	*26.3*	21.7
Portugal	19.7	19.7	19.0	20.1	28.2	*21.3*	27.2	29.5	31.4	31.6	29.6	. . .	. . .	. . .
Spain	24.7	23.3	21.8	21.0	19.9	*22.1*	18.9	19.4	20.3	19.7	18.9	17.9	*19.2*	. . .
Sweden	21.5	20.9	21.2	21.1	19.4	*20.8*	19.8	20.2	19.2	18.8	18.7	18.4	*19.2*	19.0
Switzerland	27.6	24.0	20.6	20.7	21.4	*22.9*	21.8	23.8	24.1	23.1	23.3	23.3	*23.2*	23.8
United Kingdom	20.6	20.1	19.5	18.5	18.5	*19.4*	18.8	18.1	16.4	16.5	16.3	17.3	*17.2*	17.1
United States	18.4	17.0	17.2	18.4	20.1	*18.2*	20.5	19.1	18.6	17.1	. . .	. . .	. . .	. . .
Arithmetic average non-ERM	**25.4**	**25.1**	**24.2**	**24.1**	**23.8**	**24.5**	**23.4**	**23.5**	**23.8**	**23.1**	**22.6**	**20.6**	**22.0**	. . .
Standard deviation	4.7	5.1	5.0	4.9	3.9	*4.4*	3.8	3.9	4.2	4.2	3.6	2.7	*2.6*	. . .
Coefficient of variation	0.18	0.20	0.21	0.20	0.17	*0.18*	0.16	0.17	0.18	0.18	0.16	0.13	*0.12*	. . .

Source: International Monetary Fund, *International Financial Statistics*, various issues.

Appendix II
Legal Texts

I. Excerpts from Single European Act

Preamble

. . . Whereas at their Conference in Paris from 19 to 21 October 1972 the Heads of State or of Government approved the objective of the progressive realization of economic and monetary union;

—Having regard to the Annex to the conclusions of the Presidency of the European Council in Bremen on 6 and 7 July 1978 and the Resolution of the European Council in Brussels on 5 December 1978, on the introduction of the European Monetary System (EMS) and related questions, and noting that in accordance with that Resolution, the Community and the Central Banks of the Member States have taken a number of measures intended to implement monetary cooperation.

Provisions amending the Treaty establishing the European Economic Community

Section II, Subsection II—Monetary capacity

Article 20

1. A new Chapter 1 shall be inserted in Part Three, Title II of the EEC Treaty, reading as follows:

Chapter 1

Cooperation in economic and monetary policy
(Economic and Monetary Union)

Article 102 A

1. In order to ensure the convergency of economic and monetary policy which is necessary for the further development of the Community, Member States shall cooperate in accordance with the objectives of Article 104. In doing so, they shall take account of the experience acquired in co-operation within the framework of the European Monetary System (EMS) and in developing the ECU, and shall respect existing powers in this field.

2. In so far as further development in the field of economic and monetary policy necessitates institutional changes, the provisions of Article 236 shall be applicable. The Monetary Committee and the Committee of Governors of the Central Banks shall also be consulted regarding institutional changes in the monetary area.

2. Chapters 1, 2, and 3 shall become Chapters 2, 3, and 4, respectively.

(Source: Commission of the European Communities, *Bulletin of the European Communities* (Luxembourg), Supplement 2/86.)

II. Treaty Establishing the European Economic Community

Article 104

Each Member State shall pursue the economic policy needed to ensure the equilibrium of its overall balance of payments and to maintain confidence in its currency, while taking care to ensure a high level of employment and a stable level of prices.

Article 236

The Government of any Member State or the Commission may submit to the Council proposals for the amendment of this Treaty.

If the Council, after consulting the Assembly and, where appropriate, the Commission, delivers an opinion in favour of calling a conference of representatives of the Governments of the Member States, the conference shall be convened by the President of the Council for the purpose of determining by common accord the amendments to be made to this Treaty.

The amendments shall enter into force after being ratified by all the Member States in accordance with their respective constitutional requirements.

(Source: Office for Official Publications of the European Communities, *Treaties Establishing the European Communities* (Luxembourg, 1973).)

Selective Bibliography

Abraham, F., J. Abraham, Y. Lacroix-Destrée, and F. Moss, "The European Monetary System, the European Currency Unit and the Banking World," *Revue de la Banque*, Centre d'Etudes Financières (Brussels), Vol. 48, No. 2 (February 1984), pp. 5–35.

Bank of England, "The Variability of Exchange Rates: Measurement and Effects," *Quarterly Bulletin*, Bank of England (London), September 1984.

Banque Nationale de Belgique, "Le Developpment de l'ECU Privé et la Politique Monétaire," *Bulletin de la Bank Nationale de Belgique* (Brussels), Vol. 1, No. 4 (April 1986), pp. 3–32.

Camdessus, M., Excerpts from a University Lecture, *Press Review*, Bank for International Settlements (Basel), July 25, 1985.

Ciampi, C.A., "The Positive Experience with the EMS," Excerpts from a speech to the Italian Forex Club in Venice on October 23, 1983, *Press Review*, Bank for International Settlements (Basel), November 7, 1983.

Commission of the European Communities, *Annual Report* (Brussels) various issues.

———, "Communication to the Council: Programme for Liberalization of Capital Movements in the Community" (Brussels: Commission of the European Communities, 1986).

———, "The European Monetary System—Commentary, Documents," *European Economy* (Brussels), No. 3 (July 1979), pp. 65–111.

———, "Five Years of Monetary Cooperation," COM Paper (84) 125 (Brussels: Commission of the European Communities 1984).

———, "Single European Act," *Bulletin of the European Communities* (Luxembourg), Supplement 2/86.

Committee of Governors of the Central Banks of the Member States of the Banks of the European Economic Community, Press Communiqué, June 10, 1985.

———, and European Monetary Cooperation Fund, *Texts Concerning the European Monetary System*, 1985.

Deutsche Bundesbank, *Monthly Report* (Frankfurt), June 1986.

Duisenberg, W.F., "The Chemistry of International Monetary Cooperation," Speech given at the annual meeting of the European Council of Chemical Manufacturers' Federations on June 6, 1986 in The Hague, reprinted in *Auszüge aus Presseartikeln*, Deutsche Bundesbank (Frankfurt), June 13, 1986.

European Communities, *Official Journal of the European Communities* (Luxembourg), No. C 136/1 (November 11, 1970), No. L 153 (June 11, 1983), No. L 247 (September 26, 1984). No. L 290 (November 1, 1985), No. L 341 (December 12, 1985).

European Communities, European Parliament, "Report drawn up on behalf of the Commission on Economic and Monetary Affairs and Industrial Policy on the European Monetary System," Aldo Bonaccini, Rapporteur, Document A2-196/85, (January 13, 1986).

Federal Trust for Education and Research, "The Time is Ripe—The European Monetary System, the ECU, and British Policy," David Lomax, Rapporteur, (London: Federal Trust for Education and Research, 1984).

Galy, M., "Evaluation du processus d'integration monétaire au sein du système monétaire européen," *Cahiers Economiques et Monétaires*, Banque de France (Paris), No. 20 (1985), pp. 59–98.

Gleske, L., "Die Liberalisierung des Kapitalverkehrs in der EG," Speech given at the Institut für Kapitalmarktforschung on July 3, 1986 in Frankfurt, reprinted in *Auszüge aus Presseartikeln*, Deutsche Bundesbank (Frankfurt), July 9, 1986; English translation in *Press Review*, Bank for International Settlements (Basel), August 21, 1986.

Gros, D., "On the Volatility of Exchange Rates," Unpublished manuscript, International Monetary Fund, Washington, D.C., October 1986.

House of Lords, Select Committee on the European Communities, *European Monetary System*, 5th report, Session 1983–84 (London: Her Majesty's Stationary Office, 1983).

IFO-Schnelldienst, "Das Europäische Währungssystem—Erfahrungen und Perspektiven," IFO-Institut (Munich), June 1985.

Kloten, N., "Die monetäre Integration: Was steht ihr im Wege?" *Auszüge aus Presseartikeln*, Deutsche Bundesbank (Frankfurt), May 9, 1986.

Lanyi, A. and E. Suss, "Exchange Rate Variability: Alternative Measures and Interpretation," *Staff Papers*, International Monetary Fund (Washington), Vol. 29 (December 1982), pp. 527–60.

"L'Avenir de L'ECU," 10ᵉ Journeés d'Etudes du Bischenberg 1984, *Eurépargne* (Luxembourg), No. 8–9 (August/September 1984).

Loehnis, A., "The EMS: A Central Banking Perspective," Speech given at the Federal Trust Conference "The Time is Ripe" on June 19, 1985, reprinted in *Auszüge aus Presseartikeln*, Deutsche Bundesbank (Frankfurt), July 3, 1985.

Masera, R.S., "An Increasing Role of the ECU: A Character in Search of a Script," Unpublished manuscript, Rome, April 1986.

Matthes, H., "Issues of European Monetary Integration," *Intereconomics* (Hamburg), July-August 1985, pp. 159–67.

Mayer, H.W., "Private ECUs—Potential Macro-Economic Policy Dimensions," *Economic Papers*, Bank for International Settlements (Basel), No. 16 (April 1986).

Micossi, S., "The Intervention and Financing Mechanisms of the EMS and the Role of the ECU," *Quarterly Review*, Banca Nazionale del Lavoro (Rome), December 1985, pp. 405–24.

O'Cofaigh, Tomas F., Speech given at the annual congress of Forex International in Dublin on May 31, 1986, *Press Review*, Bank for International Settlements (Basel), July 4, 1986.

Padoa-Schioppa, T., *Money, Economic Policy and Europe* (Brussels: EC Commission European Perspectives Series, 1985).

———, "Possible Future Developments within the European Monetary System and the Associated Difficulties," Excerpts from a lecture before the European University Institute in Florence on February 20, 1986, *Press Review*, Bank for International Settlements (Basel), February 21, 1986.

Pöhl, K.O., "The European Monetary System," Speech given before the Association Française des Banques on July 1, 1985, *Press Review*, Bank for International Settlements (Basel), July 8, 1985.

———, "The European Monetary System and the Outlook for the International Monetary System," Address in Rome given on April 17, 1986, *Press Review*, Bank for International Settlements (Basel), April 23, 1986.

Presse- und Informationsamt der Bundesregierung, "Erfahrungen mit dem EWS," *Aktuelle Beiträge zur Wirtschafts- und Finanzpolitik*, No. 45, July 19, 1983.

Public Policy Centre, "The Need for an Exchange Rate Policy and the Option of Full U.K. Membership in the EMS," Unpublished manuscript, London, September 1984.

Rey, J.-J., and J. Michielsen, "European Monetary Arrangements—Their Functioning and Future," Paper presented to the SUERF Colloquium, Luxembourg, October 9–11, 1986 (to be published).

Rogoff, K., "Can Exchange Rate Predictability be Achieved Without Monetary Convergence? Evidence from the EMS," *European Economic Review* (Amsterdam), Vol. 28 (1985), pp. 93–115.

Russo, M., "Why the Time is Ripe," Lecture delivered to the Bow Group, House of Commons, Unpublished manuscript, London, May 19, 1986.

Sarcinelli, M., "The EMS and the International Monetary System: Toward Greater Stability," *Quarterly Review*, Banca Nazionale del Lavoro (Rome), March 1986, pp. 57–83.

Schmidt, H., "The European Monetary System: Proposals for Further Progress," *ECU Newsletter*, Istituto Bancario San Paolo di Torino (Turin), No. 7 (April 1985), pp. 1–15.

Scott, A., "Britain and the EMS: An Appraisal of the Report of the Treasury and Civil Service Committee," *Journal of Common Market Studies* (Oxford), Vol. XXIV, No. 3 (March 1986), pp. 188–201.

Steinherr, A., "Convergence and Coordination of Macroeconomic Policies: Some Basic Issues," *European Economy* (Brussels), No. 20 (July 1984), pp. 71–110.

Szasz, A., Lecture at the Foreign Ministry in The Hague for a Conference Organized by the Interdisciplinary Study Group on European Integration, reprinted in *Auszüge aus Presseartikeln*, Deutsche Bundesbank (Frankfurt), June 13, 1986.

Tanzi, V., and T. Ter-Minassian, "The European Monetary System and Fiscal Policies," Paper presented to the Conference on Tax Coordination in the EC held in Rotterdam, August 22–24, 1985 (forthcoming).

Thomsen, J., *EMS—det europaeiske monetaere system* (Copenhagen: Nyt Nordisk Forlag Arnold Busck, 1986).

Thygesen, N., "Exchange Rate Policies and Monetary Targets in the EMS Countries," in *Europe's Money: Problems of European Monetary Co-ordination and Integration*, ed. by R.S. Masera and R. Trittin (Oxford: Clarendon Press, 1984), pp. 262–86.

Treasury and Civil Service Committee, *The European Monetary System*, Vol. I, Report (HC 57-IV); Vol. II, Minutes of Evidence (HC 57-V); Memoranda (HC 57-II, III), London 1985.

———, *International Monetary Arrangements*, Vol. I–III, London 1983.

———, *Memoranda on International Monetary Arrangements*, London 1982.

Ungerer, H., "Das Europäische Währungssystem und das internationale Wechselkurssystem" in *Geldwertstabilität und Wirtschaftswachstum*, ed. by H. Seidel, (Göttingen: Vandenhoeck and Ruprecht, 1984), pp. 97–113.

———, O. Evans, and P. Nyberg, *The European Monetary System: The Experience, 1979–82*, Occasional Paper No. 19 (Washington: International Monetary Fund, 1983), May 1983.

Walsh, B.M., "Ireland and the European Monetary System," *ECU Newsletter*, Istituto Bancario San Paolo di Turino (Turin), No. 3 (December 1983), pp. i–xxiv.

Walters, A., *Britain's Economic Renaissance* (New York: Oxford University Press, 1986).

Wegner, M., "Das EWS—ein Teilerfolg," *IFO-Schnelldienst*, 17–18/85, pp. 15–25.

Werner, P., Rapport au conseil et à la commission concernant la réalisation par étapes de l'union économique et monétaire dans la Communauté, du groupe placé sous la présidence de Monsieur Pierre Werner, *Official Journal of the European Communities* (Luxembourg), No. C 136/1 (November 11, 1970).

Ypersele, J. and J.-C. Koeune, *The European Monetary System* (Brussels: EC Commission European Perspectives Series, 1985).

Zis, G., "The European Monetary System 1979–84: An Assessment," *Journal of Common Market Studies* (Oxford), Vol. XXIII, No. 1 (September 1984), pp. 45–72.